KU-530-486

Contents

Preface

This book was commissioned by Age Concern England, which was keen that business should be made aware of the market opportunities arising from the ageing of the population. We were pleased to take on the task of writing the book because we share the belief that new horizons could indeed open up for the corporate sector if it better understood the wants and needs of older consumers.

This book brings together the essential information on four key topics, orientated towards the private sector executive or professional interested in new market opportunities:

- demographics – the way the structure of the population is projected to change over the next 20 years and beyond;

- the characteristics of older people – income, expenditure, wealth, health, disability, activity, relationships;

- design and technology, both to extend the scope of mass market products and to facilitate new specialist items to tackle the problems of ageing;

- marketing to people 50 and over.

The extent and quality of the available information and evidence are variable. The data on demographics and finance are pretty solid, but what is known about marketing is inevitably less firmly based. We have intentionally not burdened the text with precise citations to sources, but have provided short sections of 'Further reading' for readers who wish to pursue topics in greater depth.

Our subject is the market for people 50 and over, the mature market, the grey market, the silver market – call it what you will. We have set down both what is known and what seems reasonably likely, together with more speculative material where this suggests insights and potentially fruitful actions. We have not been afraid to exercise our own judgement or to offer our own ideas for consideration. We are, after all, old enough ourselves to empathise with our fellow mature consumers.

The state of understanding of the mature market is not well developed, compared with other market sectors. We hope that this book, by setting down what is known at present, will prompt further research of all kinds – market research, design research, business research, social science research – that will lead to a better understanding of the wants and needs of older people and how these can better be met. We plan to play our part in carrying forward this effort through the Older Richer Fitter project – see www.OlderRicherFitter.org.uk.

David Metz and Michael Underwood
Autumn 2004

About the authors

David Metz has been concerned with the subject of ageing for the past seven years, as director of an initiative to stimulate multi-disciplinary research, as a partner in the consultancy Population Ageing Associates, as a visiting professor in the Centre for Ageing and Public Health at the London School of Hygiene & Tropical Medicine, and as a non-executive director of a primary care trust. Earlier in his career he was a civil servant administrator and scientist in a number of Whitehall departments, and a biomedical scientist on the staff of the Medical Research Council. As well as being scientifically qualified, he is an alumnus of the London Business School.

Michael Underwood has long been interested in designing products to meet the needs of their users. In the last eight years this interest has been focused towards older and disabled people. Up to this point, his career was in the information and communications industry, where he had a variety of strategic and line-management roles in research, advanced development and design. He has direct first-hand experience of formulating and managing national multi-disciplinary research programmes, and spent a period as an expert to the European Commission advising on technology research for disabled and older people. He is also a partner in Population Ageing Associates.

Acknowledgements

The authors take full responsibility for the content of this book. They are grateful to a number of colleagues for helpful information and advice:

James Banks, Roger Coleman, Judith Cork, Robert Diamond, Alex Docherty, Lindsey Etchell, Adrian Gallop, Crawford Hollingworth, Vaughan Kennedy, Kevin Lavery, Des Le Grys, Chris Mitchell, Ann Parr, Linda Pickard, Brian Ridsdale, Jo Rigby, Dick Stroud, Isabelle Szmigin, Monica Threlfall, Mary Underwood, Matthew Wakefield, Anne Ward, Elizabeth Langton Way.

The following are gratefully acknowledged for permission to reproduce material:

Institute of Fiscal Studies, for Table 2.2

Dr Bea Steenbekkers and Delft University Press, for Figure 4.1

Crown copyright material (Table 2.1) is reproduced with the permission of the Controller of HMSO

1 Demographics

The most significant population development over the coming 50 years is certain to be a marked ageing of the population. This phenomenon of 'population ageing' is the result of three main influences: people are living longer; the baby boom generation is getting older; and the average number of children per family is declining.

Increasing longevity

In Britain, longevity has been increasing since about 1800 as measures to improve public health and to treat disease have had a growing impact. Two hundred years ago, when large numbers were dying in childhood and during childbirth, life expectancy at birth was around 35 years and less than 10 per cent of the population was aged 60 or over. By 1900, average life expectancy at birth had risen to 48 years for men and 52 years for women. Nevertheless, in 1900 over a third of all deaths were in the under-5s and barely more than 10 per cent in the over-75s, whereas today fewer than 1 in 100 deaths are in the under-5s and nearly 60 per cent in the over-75s.

With the diseases of childhood now essentially vanquished, and with increasing progress in dealing with the illnesses of mid-life, attention is now focused on the prospects for tackling ill-health in later life. Perhaps more important than treating ill-health once it has arisen is preventing it from arising in the first place. It is increasingly recognised that what is crucial for health in later life is what might be termed 'clean living' – eating a balanced diet, avoiding being overweight, exercising, not smoking, and staying mentally active and socially engaged. The signs are that this message is gradually percolating through society. The adoption of a healthy lifestyle is the clearest contributing factor to increasing longevity. The average length of life that men can expect once they have reached the age of 65 is currently increasing at the rate of 1.5 years per decade – that is, for every ten years that pass, the average man reaching age 65 can expect to live one and a half years longer. For women, the figure is one year for every decade.

But there are countervailing forces, in particular the ready availability and widespread consumption of affordable fast food, giving rise to fears of an epidemic of obesity and its associated diseases. It is increasingly recognised that health and survival in later life depend on events earlier in life. So the increase in obesity in both younger and older people could slow or even halt the trend to increasing longevity.

Expectation of life varies with social class. In England and Wales, professional men at the age of 65 can expect on average to live a further 17.5 years, while an unskilled working man can anticipate only 13.4 years. For women, the figures are 20.8 and 16.3 years respectively. These substantial disparities in part reflect differences in 'health-seeking' behaviours, particularly the tendency of the professionals to avoid smoking – the most important single cause of ill-health and early death.

Some demographers are very optimistic about future prospects for longevity, arguing that half the girls born today will probably become centenarians and half the boys should reach the age of 95. Others are less sanguine, suggesting that there must be diminishing returns to medical advances and lifestyle improvement. Official British projections of life expectancy have recently been raised, reflecting falling mortality rates. Life expectancy at birth for men is currently 76 years and is projected to rise to 81 years by 2030; for women from 80.5 to 85 years. The average expectation of life for men aged 65 is currently 16 years (ie on average a 65-year-old man can expect to live to 81) and is projected to increase to 20 years by 2030. For women aged 65, they currently can expect to live a further 19 years on average, a figure projected to increase to 23 years by 2030.

These latest British projections of longevity fall well short of the most optimistic expectations of some experts. However, most actuaries and demographers have tended to underestimate the increase in life expectancy that has actually come about. For the future, not only do we have the prospect of lifestyle improvements beyond those presently allowed for in the official projections but we also may benefit from advances in medicine. What is sometimes known as 'anti-ageing medicine' is at present more a hope than a reality (as we discuss in Chapter 8), but it would be foolish to discount entirely the possibility of important advances that will have a significant impact on the longevity of future generations.

Baby boom

The second important factor underlying the ageing population is the 'baby boom' generation – products of the post-war surge in family size. The baby boomers are ageing and will in time become a large generation of older people.

The baby boom concept has rather different meanings in different places. In the USA, the birth rate rose rapidly immediately after World War II, stayed high through the 1950s, and declined through the 1960s. In Britain there was also a rapid rise in births after the war's end, but this fell away in the late 1940s and early 1950s, probably a result of the difficult economic climate. But then, in the mid-1950s, births took off again, reaching a peak in 1964 with over a million births a year before bottoming out in 1977 at around 650,000 births a year and thereafter fluctuating between 700,000 and 800,000. So in Britain we had a two-stage baby boom, the peak of the main component coming a decade after the peak of the US boom. This means that in the USA the first of the boomers are already in their mid to late 50s, approaching or already in retirement, whilst in the UK this leading edge is still only in middle age. We need to bear in mind this difference when reading across from American experience. We should also be open to the possibility that we could learn from US experience about how this generation behaves as consumers in retirement, despite the differences in national backgrounds.

The effect of the baby boom of the late 1950s and early 1960s was to raise by about a million (about 8 per cent) relative to the surrounding generations the number of people in Britain entering work in the mid-1970s to early 1980s. They will be reaching their 50s ten years or so from now, and retirement in the 2020s. This exit from the labour market will reduce labour supply and increase the number of pensioners.

Falling fertility ● ● ● ● ● ● ● ● ● ● ● ● ● ●

The proverbial average British family of not so long ago comprised two parents and 2.4 children. This was well above the level of 2.1 children per woman needed to maintain a stable population. However, the long-term trend in fertility (the number of children per 100,000 of the population) has been downwards. Since around 1880 the birth rate has been falling, with the exception of limited increases during the baby boom. The ready availability of effective contraception and the growth of career opportunities for women have been important in sustaining the trend. The expansion of higher education is also relevant, because women with higher education qualifications start families on average five years later than those having lower educational qualifications. Later entry to motherhood is associated with the slower arrival of a second child and with fewer children over all. In Britain at present, the average number of children per woman of child-bearing age is about 1.7. In some European countries comparable family size is much lower – 1.2 children per woman in Italy and Spain, for instance.

Projections of future fertility are very uncertain. Demographers debate the prospects. Half think very low birth rates are a transient phenomenon and expect a rise to approaching 2 children per woman within a decade or two. The other half thinks low fertility rates of between 1 and 1.5 are likely to persist. Official British population projections assume a small rise to 1.8. No demographer argues that fertility in Britain is likely to rise to levels that would imply a significant natural growth to the population, let alone a repeat baby boom.

Age shift ● ● ● ● ● ● ● ● ● ● ● ● ● ● ● ●

These three factors – increasing longevity, the ageing of the baby boomers and declining fertility – are the drivers of population ageing – the 'Age Shift' as it's sometimes called. Under their influence the number of people aged 65 and over has increased by 50 per cent since 1960, from 6 million then to 9 million now. The number of over-65s is projected to hold steady until 2007, but then to grow rapidly to reach 12.5 million by 2020 as the baby boomers reach retirement, with a peak of over 16 million during the 2030s. This growth in the number of older people will take place in the context of a relatively stable total population of 60–65 million, where any overall change is likely to be the result of net inward migration.

This contemporary ageing of the population can be seen as occurring in the middle of a long-term demographic transition, from a society in which most people are young to one in which the proportion of older people is substantial. Through the course of British history, until around 1800, the proportion of those aged 60 and above did not exceed 10 per cent. Currently the figure is 21 per cent and is projected to rise to 26 per cent by 2020 and to over 30 per cent before stabilising.

The numbers of *older old* people are projected to increase at a faster rate, with those 75 and over more than doubling from today's 4.5 million to over 9 million by 2050. If half a century seems rather far ahead for forecasting, remember that all those who will be 75 or over by the middle of the century have already been born. So uncertainties about future fertility do not enter into the equation. Death rates are of course relevant and, as already noted, tend to be underestimated. The number of centenarians will also rise markedly, from 8,000 currently to perhaps 80,000 by 2040.

Women live longer than men. At birth, women currently can expect to live for 80.5 years on average, men for 76 years. This means that women outnumber men in the older age groups. The ratio of women to men is close to one until the age of 60, then rises steadily to reach 3 by the age of 90.

There is no generally agreed definition of when old age begins. Indeed, as is argued in Chapter 4, there are good reasons to avoid definitions based on chronological age. On the other hand, it seems reasonable to suppose that when people reach their 50s they begin to think about the implications of getting old – for work, leisure, income, health and so on. When thinking about the business implications of population ageing, the over-50s might be seen as the broad target market whose needs and wants are to be addressed. The key message from demography is that the over-50s are growing in numbers, from just under 20 million currently to a projected 25 million in 2020. By 2020 half of the adults in Britain will be over the age of 50, with the 'centre of gravity' continuing its upward shift thereafter. In contrast, the number of those under 50 is projected to be static, or perhaps decline slightly, over the period to 2020.

While the number of older people grows, the numbers of the young stay fairly stable or fall somewhat. The 2001 Census showed for the first time that there are more people over the age of 60 than there are children. In a UK population of 59 million, 11.9 million were younger than 16, while 12.2 million were aged 60 and over. Over the next 20 years, the size of the 15–29 age group is projected to stay fairly stable at around 11 million, while the 30–44 age group will shrink a little, from 13.5 million in 2002 to about 12 million by around 2020.

Young people and older people are not spread evenly across the country, however. Migration affects the local age structure. For instance, Inner London is a strong draw for people in their 20s, who come to study and work in the capital, both from others parts of Britain and from abroad. In contrast, the seaside towns of the south coast and the pleasant market towns of East Anglia, for instance, attract people entering retirement. In terms of markets there are marked local concentrations of older people, as can readily be seen from published data from the 2001 Census, which shows details for each local authority.

Family structure ● ● ● ● ● ● ● ● ● ● ● ●

As well as shifting the balance between young and old, low fertility and increasing longevity have implications for family structure. Perhaps the prospect of an increasingly long life ahead is a factor in the delay in the timing of key life transitions, including leaving the parental home, first marriage and the birth of the first child. The mean age of women bearing their first child in Britain is currently 29 years, which is the highest in the European Union and has increased by two years since 1990. For financial as well as demographic reasons, younger people are tending to defer many of those transitions that demonstrate a commitment to full adulthood – full economic independence from parents, formal adult union through marriage, and parenting. Some social scientists suggest that this reflects the shift from traditional societies with both high fertility and mortality to modern societies in which both are low.

Low fertility and mortality result in an increase in the number of living generations and a decrease in the number of living relatives within these generations. In the past, the typical family structure used to be 'horizontal' – people commonly had many brothers, sisters and cousins but few living grandparents. In the future, families will have a 'vertical' feel, with few siblings and cousins but four or even five generations living contemporaneously. The picture is complicated by divorce, remarriage and the growth of non-marital partnerships, bringing a greater variety of relationships. The implications for support mechanisms within families – for younger children and the frail old – remain to be seen.

Increased longevity means longer marriages, with expectations in excess of 40 years for the great majority, if not terminated by divorce. Child–parent relationships shift from being based on dependence to becoming an adult experience, with 60 years of joint life – 20 as dependant, 40 as adult. For women, time spent as daughter of a parent over the age of 65 may now exceed time spent as parent of a child under 18 – although of course 65 is not what it once was. The prospect of long marriage with a spouse chosen when young may be one of the reasons for the increase in divorce, which brings with it singles in mid-life and beyond, mature dating, late marriages and old parents.

Implications of the age shift ● ● ● ● ● ● ● ● ● ●

The prospect of population ageing prompts a number of anxieties: the adequacy of pensions; the possible need to work for longer; the availability of health and social care for the frail old; and the competitiveness of our economy. Some of these are matters of current political and public concern, and the others will become so.

What is known as the 'support ratio' is the number of people in the population aged 15–64 as a proportion of the number aged 65 and over. Currently the support ratio is 4, and is forecast to fall to 2.1 by 2040 if fertility stays at the recent level of 1.6 children per woman (or 2.5 if it rises to 1.8, respectively). This is a quite dramatic fall in the number of working-age people able to sustain those in retirement, and is an important influence in the debate underway about whether to raise the retirement age.

We should, however, keep in the forefront of our minds the fact that long healthy life is one of the main achievements of our civilisation. The central concern of this book is how the needs and wants of an ageing population may be recognised and met, and how business may be built on the demographic age shift now underway.

The key points for the corporate sector as regards the age shift are that:

■ the centre of gravity of the population is shifting upwards significantly;

■ the number of people 50 and over in the UK is projected to rise from the current 20 million to 25 million in 20 years' time;

■ by 2020, people 50 and over will comprise half the adult population;

■ the numbers in younger age groups are projected to be static or decline.

Further reading

Arber, S. and Ginn, J. (2004) 'Ageing and gender: diversity and change', *Social Trends 34*. London: The Stationery Office

Census 2001. London: Office of National Statistics

Government Actuary's Department, United Kingdom Population Projections 2002-based, December 2003

Harper, S. (2003) *Changing Families as Societies Age*. Oxford: Institute of Ageing, research report RR103

Office of National Statistics (1999) *Social Focus on Older People*. London: The Stationery Office

Shaw, C. (2001) 'United Kingdom population trends in the 21st century', *Population Trends* vol 103, Spring

2 Income, wealth and purchasing power

Until fairly recently, older people were generally seen as among the poorer members of society, having the ability to acquire only the more basic goods and services. They were therefore not viewed as an attractive consumer market. There have been considerable changes in recent years in the financial position of older people, of course, as incomes from occupational pensions have risen for a large proportion of the retired population. The economic well-being of older people depends not only on income but also on property assets and financial wealth, and these too have grown.

Income

Thirty years ago pensioners comprised nearly half the households with income below the conventional poverty threshold of 60 per cent of the median household income. (The *median* household income is the middle value when the incomes of all households are set out from lowest to highest. The median is lower than the mean or average income, because the latter is boosted by the relatively small number of high-income households.)

Nowadays, in contrast, less than a quarter of pensioner households are below the poverty line on this definition. So poverty has become less concentrated in the post-retirement years. This improvement in the position of older people is a result of the growth of occupational and private pensions and the build-up of the earnings-related component of the state pension system. The result is that the rate of poverty among pensioners is now roughly the same as that among most non-pensioner groups. Compared with average incomes among non-pensioners, average pensioner incomes are now higher than at any time in the last 40 years.

It is perhaps unexpected to find that retirement does not in general imply a marked reduction in either income or expenditure. The ratio of average income post-retirement to that pre-retirement is known as the *income replacement rate*. For the developed economies generally, the replacement rate is in the range 75–85 per cent, with Britain at the bottom end of this band. Another basis for comparison is the average pensioner income in relation to the average income of the whole population, adjusted for household size. The ratio for Britain is 78 per cent, compared with an average of 83 per cent for 15 developed countries. These cross-country comparisons suggest that pensioners in the UK do about as well on average – relative to society as a whole – as their counterparts in other developed countries. Bearing in mind the savings in work-related expenses, such as travel to work, and the likely completion of mortgage repayments, most people should not experience a material fall in living standards through the retirement transition.

This is not to suggest that everything in the garden is financially rosy during retirement. Although the current generation of people of pension age is the most affluent ever – the result of a continuous rise in average income from occupational pensions and benefits – there remains significant poverty in old age, some 2 million pensioners living in low-income households.

Welfare benefits, including the state pension, account for at least half the income of some 70 per cent of pensioners, and for 15 per cent these make up their entire income. Pensioners may be entitled to a wide range of benefits. Those on low incomes can claim the Pension Credit, as well as Council Tax Benefit and Housing Benefit. There are also disability-related benefits for those eligible. However, between a quarter and a third of entitled pensioners do not claim Pension Credit and significant numbers do not claim other benefits. The National Audit Office has estimated that between £930 million and £1,860 million of entitlements went unclaimed by pensioners in 1999/2000. This lack of take-up reflects a number of factors:

- lack of knowledge of benefit entitlement;

- confusion about benefits currently received, resulting in failure to claim full entitlement; and

- the perceived stigma that many feel is involved in receiving 'hand-outs'.

The level of Pension Credit is quite close to the 60 per cent of median income poverty threshold, so if take-up could be increased substantially there would be a big impact on reducing pensioner poverty.

There is, however, a cause of poverty in old age that is more fundamental than the failure to claim benefits. It is primarily low income during working life that prevents people from making adequate provision for old age. In essence, a person who has had a solid employment history in jobs that benefit from an occupational pension can generally expect to have a financially comfortable retirement. People with broken employment records or who have held only low-paid employment or whose earnings have been low for any other reason will be far less favourably placed. So poverty tends to perpetuate itself from working life into retirement, as does relative affluence. Women of course are particularly likely to have broken employment records and have lower earnings on average than men. So women do worse from the pension system than men. People with disabilities and members of ethnic minorities are also more likely to have low earnings and hence low incomes in retirement.

A third factor contributing to poverty in old age is age itself. Older pensioners are less well off than younger pensioners on average. Their occupational pensions, related to final salaries, were lower in real terms when they retired, and have since at best been up-rated in line with price inflation. The other side of the coin is that pensioner incomes tend to rise over time as younger, richer generations retire and older, poorer generations gradually die out. The former benefit from higher average incomes across their working life and, hence, access to higher earnings-related pension income in retirement. Moreover, the average income of a pensioner generation rises over time because better-off individuals tend to live longer, and there is increased receipt of disability benefits with age.

Let us put some numbers to these generalisations. The average income of pensioners in 2002/3 was £388 per week gross for couples and £203 for single pensioners. This includes income from all sources. The effect of increasing age is significant. As shown in Table 2.1, recently retired pensioners (within five years of state pension age) are better off than those where the head of household is under the age of 75, who in turn are better off than older pensioners.

	Couples	Single
Recently retired	£438	£246
Head of household under 75	£417	£218
Head of household 75+	£336	£190

Table 2.1 Average income of pensioners in 2001/2

There is also a significant gender effect. For single men the average gross weekly income is £221 while for single women it is £197.

It is interesting to compare these average incomes with estimates published in 2002 by the Family Budget Unit on the cost of maintaining a 'modest but adequate' living standard for households aged 65–74, including taxes. This standard was judged to be what most households would aim at, well above the poverty threshold but well short of affluence. Six different household types were assessed, based on people living in York, which was considered representative of Britain as a whole. The estimated budgets fell in the range £157–204 per week for single people without a car and £233–277 for couples without a car. There was little difference between men and women but tenants needed more income than owner-occupiers. Car ownership required £25–30 per week over and above the basic budgets.

Taking the figures for pensioner income and 'modest but adequate' budgets together, it is apparent that, *on average*, even older pensioner couples could afford this living standard, including a car.

However, the position of single pensioners is less favourable. Age Concern has estimated that 80 per cent of single tenants could not afford this modest but adequate living standard, based on present incomes. In part this is due to the failure of many pensioners to take up benefits to which they are entitled.

As always when discussing older people, it is important to bear in mind the range that lies behind the average. The span of pensioner incomes is almost as wide as that for the population as a whole. Pensioners are relatively over-represented in the 2nd, 3rd, 4th and 5th lowest decile groups of the overall income distribution (a *decile* is one-tenth of the population distributed in this case by income, from lowest to highest). However, pensioners are *under-*represented in the 1st (or very lowest) decile, the bottom 10 per cent of income distribution. Moreover, as many as 40 per cent of pensioner couples and 36 per cent of single pensioners are to be found in the top half of the income distribution.

The incomes of pensioners generally are now more favourable than they have been in the past, both in absolute terms and relative to the population as a whole. What of the future? As society gets richer, one might hope that retirement incomes would continue to grow and that remaining pensioner poverty could be eliminated. But that is hardly how matters appear at the moment, with very many final-salary-related occupational pension schemes closing to new members, some even closing to further contributions from existing members, the value of financial assets well down from their peak, and with the funds from money-purchase pensions buying lower levels of annuity income than in the recent past.

The current generation of the recently retired – sometimes characterised as the 'golden generation' – have benefited from extraordinarily high asset returns that are unlikely to be repeated, from bequests from parents who have not lived long enough to use up their assets, from growth in defined benefit occupational pension schemes paying out pensions worth up to two-thirds of final salary, and from high levels of home ownership. It is widely supposed that future retirees will face greater uncertainty about their level of retirement income, following the shift towards defined contribution pension schemes in which the risks are assumed by the employee and not the employer.

The Financial Services Authority has summarised the wealth-related characteristics of successive generations:

- **over-70s:** many, particularly older women, have no financial wealth at all. There are considerable inequalities in income, more than 40 per cent of those aged 75 and over receiving some income-related benefits from the state. For many in this generation their most significant asset is their home, more than half owning their property outright.

- **60s:** many have benefited from growth in occupational pension schemes. Levels of home ownership and equity ownership are higher than for the previous generation.

- **50s:** the post-war baby boom, likely to benefit from a further increase in pensioner income as they move into retirement. The majority will have belonged to occupational pension schemes, and women are more likely to have a pension in their own right. Levels of home ownership and equity ownership are higher than before.

- **40s and under:** likely to be affected by a shift to defined contribution pensions, hence greater uncertainty about income in retirement, which is not certain to be higher than that of their predecessors.

For future generations of pensioners, much depends on the length of working life. One reason why established pension arrangements are under pressure is that life expectancy is increasing unexpectedly quickly, as discussed in Chapter 1. Pension schemes have therefore to pay out for longer than was planned when contributions from employees and employers were calculated and investment return targets adopted. So the sums set aside during working life now need to be spread over a longer period of retirement, meaning a lower level of annual income. One possible response to this, which is gaining increasing recognition, would be to increase the effective age of retirement proportionately to the increase in average longevity, to preserve the balance between working and non-working life. Of course, this would not be popular with many of those at present in the later phases of working life who are looking forward to a well-earned retirement. So we may expect to see measures that encourage a longer working life, with any changes to the age of receipt of the state pension phased in over a fairly long period, as is happening with women's entitlement to the state pension, the age for which will rise from 60 to 65 over the period 2010 to 2020.

We noted above that all the developed countries achieve a similar outcome in terms of the ratio of pension income to working income, despite very different financing arrangements for pensions. This suggests that a replacement rate of around 80 per cent reflects a fairly deeply held desire within developed societies, which is quite likely to hold in the future. No doubt new pensions and savings mechanisms may be needed, as well as suitable legislative and regulatory frameworks. Nevertheless, when thinking about the income and wealth of current and future generations of those entering retirement, we need not be pessimistic in our outlook.

Expenditure

Most personal income is devoted to expenditure on goods and services. From the viewpoint of this book, the main reason to consider pensioner income, as we have, is to get a sense of the spending power of this major segment of the population.

The Office of National Statistics has carried out an annual survey of household expenditure since 1957. It was originally called the Family Expenditure Survey but has recently been combined with the survey of food consumption and renamed the Expenditure and Food Survey. Table 2.2 shows household expenditure by the age of the head of household and by category of expenditure (extensive further details are published for expenditure within each category). It will be seen that total average weekly expenditure per household falls as age increases, from £451 for the 50–64 age group to £177 for the 75 and over age group. Part of this is due to smaller household size (2.2 and 1.4 persons respectively), and part to lower incomes. It is noteworthy that the average weekly expenditure *per person* is £157 for the age group 65–74 compared with £202 for those 50–64. The former is 78 per cent of the latter, close to the analogous income replacement rate discussed earlier. If housing and transport costs are disregarded (because typically mortgages are paid off around retirement, and the cost of travel to work no longer arises), then expenditure by the 65–74 age group is 85 per cent of that of the 50–64 age group. These expenditure data confirm that for the majority there is no step change downwards in material standards when an individual retires.

Age group	30–49	50–64	65–74	75+
Food and non-alcoholic drink	48.20	47.80	37.90	29.40
Alcohol, tobacco	13.00	13.40	8.50	5.10
Clothing, footwear	29.20	24.00	11.60	7.80
Housing, fuel and power	38.90	35.30	29.30	25.90
Household goods and services	35.70	36.90	22.00	14.90
Health	4.60	6.30	5.90	3.50
Transport	72.90	72.40	35.10	15.60
Communication	12.80	10.60	6.90	5.10
Recreation, culture	67.10	65.60	42.10	23.00
Education	7.40	6.94	1.00	–
Restaurants, hotels	44.00	38.50	20.10	11.50
Miscellaneous goods and services	41.20	34.70	22.20	16.90
Other expenditure*	82.10	59.30	27.40	17.80
Total expenditure £ pw	**496.90**	**451.40**	**270.90**	**177.20**
Average number of persons per household	3.0	2.2	1.7	1.4
Average weekly expenditure *per person*	165.60	202.50	157.30	122.60

* 'Other expenditure' includes mortgage interest and holidays.

(From Table 2.1 of *Family Spending 2002/03*, Office of National Statistics, London.)

Table 2.2 Average weekly household expenditure (£) by age of head of household, 2002/3

Overall annual expenditure of people aged 50 and over amounts to around £175 billion a year. This represents about 45 per cent of total household expenditure.

Expenditure patterns change with age, however. As people get older, they spend proportionately less on transport, alcohol, tobacco, clothing, restaurants, holidays and mortgage interest payments, and proportionately more on housing, fuel and power, and on food and non-alcoholic drinks. These differences reflect changes in both obligations (eg children having flown the nest, no travel to work, or the mortgage paid off) and in priorities within constrained overall budgets, as well as in changing tastes. It needs to be borne in mind that the expenditure patterns shown in Table 2.2 are those of different generations. It should not be assumed that, as the 50–64 age group ages, its consumption pattern would be exactly the same as for the present 65–74 generation.

The expenditure data include spending on consumer durables. But here, accumulated stocks are important for standards of living. Those now retiring will almost invariably have a telephone, television, central heating, washing machine and fridge-freezer. Ownership rates of video and CD players and for microwave ovens are well over 50 per cent for pensioner couple households (rather lower for singles), although levels of ownership decline with increasing age. People often replace consumer durables at around the time of their retirement, taking advantage of the lump sum from an occupational pension. In the past, this might have been seen as an investment to 'see me through' – that is, to last for the remainder of the time during which the purchaser lived in their own home. Nowadays, however, with increasing longevity, there may be a need for subsequent replacement – the *late replacement market* – at which time the onset of disability may prompt a particular interest in inclusively designed appliances, as discussed in Chapter 6.

The expenditure data include spending on home maintenance. Sixty per cent of pensioners at present are owner-occupiers, a proportion expected to grow to 80 per cent as the next generation enters retirement. However, a consequence is that the main part of substandard owner-occupied housing is that of pensioners whose incomes are inadequate to maintain their properties.

Savings ● ● ● ● ● ● ● ● ● ● ● ● ● ● ●

Any excess of income over expenditure (and giving) results in saving. Elementary economic theory suggests that people should save during their working life and draw on their savings during retirement. That, of course, is the basis of money-purchase pension schemes. It is also the logic of paying off your mortgage while working and enjoying the benefit of rent-free accommodation in retirement. Nevertheless, contrary to theory, on average people continue to save throughout later life by putting aside some part of their regular income.

There is a lack of good data on savings rates in Britain. However, estimates made by deducting consumption expenditure from income indicate that the peak of saving occurs in the early 50s, falls as people get older, but always remains positive. The British seem to save more in old age than do the inhabitants of other countries, perhaps due in part to habits developed earlier in life. On average, the British save 8–10 per cent of their disposable income across their lives.

Over 80 per cent of people aged 65 and over believe that it is important to save for the future. Older people may be more cautious in their expenditure because they cannot be sure how long they will survive, nor whether they will need residential care at some point. They can no longer replenish their savings by working. Hence they continue to save out of income if at all possible, 'saving for a rainy day' reported as the biggest single motivation. They may also be anxious to leave bequests to their children and grandchildren. Moreover, earlier experiences, for instance of wartime shortages and post-war rationing, may result in many adhering to rather frugal habits – a phenomenon that may be perpetuated if future pension levels disappoint.

On the other hand, there is some suggestion from recent surveys that the present generation of those newly over 50 see themselves as less inclined to hold back expenditure in order to leave an inheritance. They envisage a busy life involving expenditure on travel, holidays and active leisure pursuits. Moreover, not being in work means that becoming unemployed is no longer a risk. Whilst the pension's value may decline relatively, as earnings generally grow, once a pension starts to be paid it can nevertheless be relied upon as a secure source of income.

There is an evident tension between spending your money while you're fit and able to enjoy life, and feeling you ought to keep a good reserve in hand to deal with the unexpected. The right size of this reserve is harder to judge the further you are from the point at which you might need it.

A particular uncertainty in later life for which savings may be put aside is the possibility that the onset of frailty will require the purchase of nursing or other care, whether in the individual's own home or in residential accommodation. The typical life course involves at its end a period of frailty during which personal and nursing care is needed. Generally, people prefer to remain in their own home for as long as possible. Nevertheless, the amount of care may build up to a level where residential care is needed. The costs of this can of course be substantial. The current chances of long-stay entry into a care home at some point during the remainder of life are 20 per cent for a man aged 65 and 36 per cent for a woman of the same age. So the risks are not inconsiderable and justify putting aside savings for this possible eventuality.

Most people in care homes at present, however, are state supported, because their incomes and savings are too low for them to be self-funding. The existence of such state funding for long-term care could act as a deterrent to saving and to taking out long-term care insurance, as discussed in Chapter 8. The Pension Credit arrangements, which began in October 2003, and which guarantee a minimum level of income to everyone aged 60 and over, could also deter people from saving, because entitlement depends on savings levels as well as income. It remains to be seen whether these deterrents to savings outweigh the propensity to save noted above.

Wealth ● ● ● ● ● ● ● ● ● ● ● ● ● ● ● ● ●

The wealth of individuals is derived from accumulated savings together with any inheritance. On average, net financial wealth (excluding housing and pension wealth) increases with age to reach a peak in the mid-60s before declining. UK survey data for the year 2002 indicate that the mean value of net financial wealth per 'family unit' (single adult or cohabiting or married couple) is around £50,000 for people in their 60s, £38,000 for people in their 70s, and £30,000 for those in their 80s (see Table 2.3). The inequality of wealth distribution around these mean values is considerable, reflecting past earnings and past decisions on how much to save out of income.

Age band	Mean net financial assets*
50–54	£40,000
55–59	£54,000
60–64	£50,000
65–69	£49,000
70–74	£39,000
75–79	£37,000
80+	£30,000

* The net assets shown are per 'family unit' – ie either a single adult or cohabiting/ married couple, and any dependent children.

(From Table 3A.7 of Marmot et al (2003) *Health, wealth and lifestyles of the older population in England: the 2002 English Longitudinal Study of Ageing.*)

Table 2.3 Distribution of net financial wealth in the UK by age

Based on these survey data, the total net financial wealth of people aged 50 and over is of the order of £560 billion. This probably amounts to around 85 per cent of all such wealth.

The housing wealth of older people is also very substantial. Three-quarters of those aged 60–70 own their own home, as do 60 per cent of those over the age of 70. Most home owners have paid off their mortgage by the time they retire. The average value of net housing wealth per person over 50 is about £70,000 (or £100,000 if only owner-occupiers are counted).

A further source of information about the wealth of older people comes from the value of bequests. In aggregate, the value of estates was £34.6 billion in 1999/2000, of which £2 billion was collected as tax and £1.5 billion was left as legacies to charities. The £33 billion remaining was largely comprised of residential property (37 per cent), securities (23 per cent) and cash (23 per cent).

Given that there are about 600,000 deaths a year, it follows that the average amount of financial assets bequeathed is around £55,000. Again, this average conceals wide variations. Rather more than half of those who die leave assets worth less than £5,000, whilst over half of £34.6 billion comes from the 14 per cent of largest estates.

The large and growing scale of inheritance points to the substantial unspent wealth of older people and perhaps to a degree of 'over-saving'. The proportion of estates in the form of cash perhaps suggests the existence of imperfections in capital markets which prevent older people getting what they see as fair value for their investments.

Implications

The key implications of the main features of the income and wealth of older people outlined in this chapter can be summarised:

- Annual expenditure of people aged 50 and over amounts to around £175 billion a year. This represents about 45 per cent of total household expenditure.

- Financially, there is no great change in income or expenditure around retirement. A reduction in both by some 20 per cent on average following retirement reflects lower income offset by fewer financial obligations. New pensioners are therefore in a pretty similar position financially to late-working-age people of similar socio-economic status. They are no more likely to be poor than their somewhat younger counterparts.

- Older people generally continue to save throughout retirement, accumulating substantial net financial wealth as well as housing wealth. The financial net wealth of people aged 50 and over is more than £500 billion.

- Having accumulated the basic consumer durables, older people may be reluctant to replace these unless it is unavoidable, despite most having the income that would allow them to do so. In terms of consumption, many older people do not enjoy the living standards they could well afford. There may therefore be opportunities for marketing goods that would be seen as excellent value for money and services that provide unique lifetime experiences (such as a once-in-a-lifetime cruise).

- The scale of bequests also argues for the possibility that older people save more than they need. The amount of cash left as bequests suggests marketing opportunities for low-risk savings schemes.

- Although the financial position of older people generally has been improving, there remain many poorer pensioners, in part because of £1–2 billion a year of state benefits not taken up. Is there an ethical and viable business opportunity to provide advice on entitlements? (This aspect is considered in Chapter 8.)

Further reading

Banks, J., Smith, Z. and Wakefield, M. (2002) *The Distribution of Financial Wealth in the UK: evidence from 2000 BHPS data*. WP02/21. London: Institute for Fiscal Studies

Bebbington, A., Darton, R. and Netten, A. (1997) *Lifetime Risk of Entering Residential or Nursing Home Care in England*. Discussion paper 1230/3. Canterbury: Personal Social Services Research Unit, University of Kent

Department for Work and Pensions. *Family Resources Survey 2001–2002*. London: DWP

Department for Work and Pensions. (2004) *Pensioners' Income Series 2002/03*. London: DWP, Pensions Analysts Division

Disney, R. and Johnson, P. (eds). (2002) *Pensions Systems and Retirement Incomes across OECD Countries*. Cheltenham: Edward Elgar

Financial Services Authority. (2002) *Financing the Future: mind the gap*. London: FSA

Financial Services Authority. (2002) *Impact of an Ageing Population for the FSA*. London: FSA

Goodman, G., Myck, M. and Shepherd, A. (2003) *Sharing the Nation's Prosperity? Pensioner poverty in Britain*. Commentary 93. London: Institute for Fiscal Studies

Marmot, M., Banks, J., Blundell, R. et al (eds). (2003) *Health, Wealth and Lifestyles of the Older Population in England: the 2002 English Longitudinal Study of Ageing*. London: Institute of Fiscal Studies

Office of National Statistics. (2002) *Family Spending: Expenditure and Food Survey, 2002/03*. London: Office for National Statistics/The Stationery Office

Organisation for Economic Cooperation and Development. (2001) *Ageing and Income – financial resources in 9 OECD countries*. Paris: OECD

Parker, H. (2002) *Modest but Adequate – a reasonable living standard for households aged 65–74 years*; Family Budget Unit, University of York. London: Age Concern England

Pensions Policy Institute. (2003) *Why are Older Pensioners Poorer?* Briefing Note Number 6. London: PPI

3 Changing ideas of ageing

Designing and marketing products and services suited to older consumers requires a good understanding of the target market. There are two elements to this understanding: the facts and the ideas. In the next chapter we look at the facts – what characterises older people. In this chapter we review the main ideas about ageing and the meaning of old age.

Until the latter part of the 20th century, old age had been viewed mainly as a biological and medical phenomenon. With the passage of the years our physiological and psychological competences tend to decline. This leads to the ailments of old age, which prompt medical interventions, commonly resulting in simultaneous intake of many prescribed medicines, as well as personal and nursing care provided both by family and by professionals. Classic social scientists paid little attention to old age and ageing. Studies of old age were limited to medical texts. However, in recent years the field of social gerontology has become quite active, involving research to collect data on behaviour in later life and thought about the conceptual significance and policy implications of the research findings. Indeed, some social scientists argue that ageing is a key cultural phenomenon of our times.

Theories on ageing

The first social 'theory' of ageing focused on the phenomenon of disengagement. It was argued that, as people get older, their contact with the world lessens, partly through growing disability and decline in the senses and partly through loss of spouses and friends. It was supposed that it suited older people to disengage from involvement in society in order to prepare for the ultimate disengagement caused by incapacitating disease or death. Society imposes fewer social responsibilities on older people and they surrender some of their responsibilities. In this way the disruption of society is minimised.

From a contemporary viewpoint, disengagement theory would be seen at best as offering only a very limited perspective on the current phenomenon of ageing, perhaps most relevant to individuals with a tendency to be reclusive and to those who become very frail. In this respect it is not untypical of theories in social science, which are really just ideas or generalisations that reflect a common perception and some current data. Nevertheless, such theoretical ideas are worth considering since they aim to capture some of the essence of the ageing process.

In recent decades what is known as the *structured dependency theory* has been the prevalent mode of thought in British social gerontology. The central idea is that the dependent position of older people is created by social policy. The very existence of a state pension system is seen as resulting in the marginalisation and social exclusion of older people. They become 'old age pensioners', ex-workers with no productive social role, living in relative poverty and enforced idleness. The focus of the structured dependency approach is on poorer older people and remedies to their situation through political action to influence the state, particularly to increase the basic state pension.

As pensioner poverty has lessened, and as a greater range of opportunities has opened to people after retirement from their main career, structured dependency no longer provides an adequate understanding of the main features of later life. People's lives after work have become richer and more complex, with more diversity and choice. As longevity increases and retirement takes place earlier, there are more people no longer in full-time employment, and hence more diversity, with greater access to financial, cultural and social capital. Critics of the structured dependency theory argue that, by emphasising the plight of the poor and frail in the retired population, poverty and frailty are seen as the very essence of ageing. What then tends to be neglected is information on how older people actually spend their lives, and the options open to them to choose their identities. Work-based identities may give way to consumption- or culturally-based identities after retirement.

The Third Age

The phrase 'the Third Age' captures the growing recognition of the opportunities open to people after their main period of working life is concluded. The First Age is the period of childhood and adolescence, characterised by dependence, socialisation, immaturity and education. The Second Age is the era of independence, maturity and responsibility, of earning and of saving, and of family formation. The Third Age is then the period of personal achievement and fulfilment, and is followed by the Fourth Age – final dependence and decrepitude. The four ages are not defined by the calendar nor by birthdays, but rather by economic and attitudinal factors and by health. For men the Third Age usually begins after retirement from their main full-time employment.

In this, perhaps somewhat idealised, view the life course of the individual is seen to culminate in the Third Age. The notion of 'old age' becomes obsolete. The idea of the Third Age becomes important when the number of retired people becomes substantial. So it is a fairly recent phenomenon, not becoming established as a settled feature of the social structure until the 1980s. For instance, the University of the Third Age, comprising local self-governing groups involved in teaching and learning, began in Britain in 1981.

The Third Age phenomenon can be seen as arising from the enhanced economic status that improving pension schemes have conferred on the newly retired population in recent decades. This allows continued participation in the consumer culture. At the same time, rising levels of educational attainment and cultural involvement facilitate the citizenship and social capital aspects of the Third Age, for instance through voluntary activities. The Third Age concept presumes the active construction of a post-work identity, on the basis that the pre-existing social structures of work, the family and the neighbourhood are not sufficient to enable expression of the individual's Third Age lifestyle.

Forever young? ● ● ● ● ● ● ● ● ● ● ● ● ● ●

The proposition that the Third Age is a culmination of the life course, a time of personal achievement and fulfilment, implies that people would welcome its commencement. But in fact, staying young seems to be the sentiment expressed by growing segments of the whole adult population. Resisting old age and ageing itself has become an integral component of many adult lifestyles. People are choosing not to grow old, or at least attempting to delay the onset of physical and mental decline, through the practice of 'active ageing' or 'healthy ageing'. There is an increasing emphasis on disciplining the body through virtuous nutrition and physical exercise, together with social engagement. People see getting older as the regrettable by-product of the good life of affluent early retirement, and would ideally opt for the looks and physical capability of someone 20 years younger while keeping the kind of confidence and attitude they have at present. They expect to be fitter, stronger and more confident than previous generations.

Before the 1960s, what carried cultural weight in most societies was the value system expressed through the lives of middle-aged men of the upper middle classes. We generally looked up to our elders, deferred to their wisdom and experience, and hoped for a career involving progression to such seniority. Recall those Victorian group portraits of politicians or the military, with the younger men attempting to look decidedly mature. The arrival of youth culture and pop culture undermined all that. Now we seemingly aspire to youth, expect respect regardless of experience, think new is good, desire instant fame, and seek jobs not careers. Resisting the onset of old age involves staying in touch with the youth culture, rejecting both the marginalisation of pensioner status and the comforts of the Third Age. So, although the demographic centre of gravity of society (as measured by median age) is shifting, it doesn't feel like that. The transition to adulthood has changed – people become 'grown up' sooner but stay young for longer, postponing full independence from parental support and the serious start of a career. This re-emphasis of youth acts to reinforce the disinclination of many mid-life and older people to 'act their age'.

Resisting ageing implies a widening discrepancy between a person's calendar or chronological age and their psychological age – their sense of how old they feel, how far they've come, how far to go. Such resistance is the more likely when the person's biological clock seems to be ticking relatively slowly – they're fit and healthy 'for their age' – so that their biological age is lower than their chronological age.

Physical ageing is, however, harder to deal with than psychological ageing, and our aspirations may be held back by physical limitations. Our sense of well-being depends on a number of factors, including our physical health, the happiness and success of our children, our spiritual beliefs and our energy. The saying 'you're only as old as you feel' has some truth but over-simplifies. We can feel partly old, partly young – depending on how such factors develop and inter-play for each individual.

Nevertheless, chronological age remains an important signifier of social and civic identity. Birthday cards make humorous references to ageing. Generation labelling is based on age: Generation X, Thirty-somethings, Baby Boomers. Age has steadily increased its hold on our thinking since registration of births became compulsory in 1836. We judge our career success, sporting prowess, health and appearance in relation to where we ought to be 'for our age'. Some commentators argue that social age is replacing social class in the way we think about the shape of our society.

Chronological age is not, however, a particularly good indicator of health status – or anything else, for that matter. Among a randomly selected group of people aged 70, say, there will be enormous variation, ranging from senior athletes to the physically frail, from the vigorously creative to the relaxed stoic, from the intellectually agile to those who are slowing down mentally. This is the reason for attempting to break down the older age group into segments when thinking about their needs and wants, as we discuss in Chapter 5.

Human diversity – the variation among people – increases with age. Conventional chronological age, counting the passage of the seasons starting from birth, is a poor guide. Better to count the months back from death, as the main need for medical and health care over the whole life course is in the final year or two. We would do better to reckon our years, as Gabriel Garcia Marquez proposed in *Love in the Time of the Cholera*, 'not in relation to the number of years they had lived, but in relation to the time left to them before they died'. But of course, counting backwards can only be done with hindsight.

Variation among older people is also the consequence of gender differences. Women experience the menopause, a biological landmark in the life course. For men, there is nothing analogous, notwithstanding the efforts of those who offer remedies to deal with the so-called 'male menopause'. Physiological functioning does indeed decline with increasing age, as is discussed in the next chapter. Socially, however, masculinity is less compromised by ageing, and men are seen as attractive partners for longer into old age by women who feel under more societal pressures to disguise their age. On the other hand, women are less subject to loss of role on retirement, and are more able to take advantage of inter-generational links, given that they tend to have the main caring responsibility in families.

Discrimination and inclusion ● ● ● ● ● ● ● ● ● ●

You might argue that it would be better to drop age altogether – to be, in a sense, 'ageless'. Let us judge people on what they can, or cannot, do, on their capabilities and disabilities, regardless of how many birthdays they have celebrated. This view underlies a number of current initiatives to ban age discrimination in its various guises. Legislation to outlaw age discrimination in employment will operate from 2006, with the possible elimination of obligatory retirement ages. The National Health Service is committed to rooting out age discrimination in the provision of health care, so that a patient's chronological age does not affect decisions on their treatment; what matters is the ability to benefit.

The positive approach to eliminating age discrimination involves taking an inclusive view, whether in employment, in the provision of goods and services or in marketing. Inclusivity means designing, planning and managing to maximise the proportion of the population for whom the service is suited. An inclusive approach treats older people simply as people, with no special regard paid to their age. As we propose in subsequent chapters, this is an important means to unlock the spending power of older customers.

The frailties and disabilities of later life are traditionally seen as characterising older people. Where medical science is able to alleviate such disabilities, this is of course to be welcomed. But we need to recognise that the impact of such disabilities depends on how the physical world in which we live is arranged. Inclusive design minimises the practical handicaps associated with disability. So, for example, well-executed directional signs in public spaces that pay attention to colour contrast, font size and shape, illumination and location, will reduce the handicap experienced by people whose vision has become impaired.

Nevertheless, there are situations where discrimination – in the positive sense – based on explicit recognition of the age of the customer group is generally sensible. In some circumstances, affinity groups form naturally, based on mutual acceptance of age. Examples include the University of the Third Age and the many cruise ships and other specialist holiday arrangements that cater for older clients, not to mention bingo, luncheon clubs and tea dances.

Implications ● ● ● ● ● ● ● ● ● ● ● ● ●

How people think about ageing has changed over time, driven partly by changes in the real world and partly by shifting views about what is ideologically and culturally important. Are ideas about the nature of ageing relevant to how one might think about the behaviour of mature consumers?

Arguably, the fundamental purpose of marketing is to restructure society in order to meet unmet needs. The structure of society includes both physical and cultural aspects. So, having a feel for both the physical and the cultural dimensions of ageing is indeed relevant to engagement with older consumers.

The latest shift of the cultural *zeitgeist* places emphasis on 'inclusivity' – including older people in the mainstream, whether in the realms of employment, design, retailing, advertising or marketing. In an inclusive world, capability is more significant than disability, and the number of years from death is more relevant than the number from birth. As the centre of gravity of society shifts away from the young, and as the 'new old' become included, the prospects for the continued dominance of the youth culture are beginning to look rather uncertain. Marketing orientated towards the young may therefore be based on increasingly shaky foundations.

Further reading

Ageing and Society (the journal of the British Society of Gerontology)

Bond, J., Coleman, P. and Peace, S. (eds). (1993) *Ageing in Society*, 2nd edition. London: Sage

Gilleard, C. and Higgs, P. (2000) *Cultures of Ageing*. Harlow: Prentice Hall

Help the Aged (2002) *Age Discrimination in Public Policy: a review of the evidence*. London: HtA

Laslett, P. (1996) *A Fresh Map of Life*, 2nd edition. Basingstoke: Macmillan

Scales, J. and Scase, R. (2000) *Fit and Fifty?* Swindon: Economic and Social Research Council

4 What's it like to be old?

With increasing longevity and the growth of more positive attitudes towards ageing, what it means to be old is perhaps less obvious than it might once have seemed. For one thing, when does 'old age' begin? When asked, people mostly mention an age more advanced than their own. Except for the very oldest, there are always people around who seem older than we are and they provide our reference point. For adults in our youth-orientated society, there is evidently no bonus in purporting to be older than we seem.

For the purposes of this book, we might say that the key decade in people's lives is their 50s. Of course, it is not that old age starts then. Rather, it's the time when most of us begin to think about being old. We know that we're past the half-way mark; retirement is in prospect; children have mostly left home; wealth has accumulated. How are we going to cope, first with an unfamiliar amount of leisure time while we are fit and then with becoming dependent when we grow frail? What are the significant aspects of the second part of our lives that determine our needs and our wants? This is the subject of the present chapter.

Bodily capabilities

However young we may feel, our health is very likely to deteriorate, eventually, with advancing age. Either we become ill with a particular disease or we become frail as the consequence of the combination of multiple minor impairments. But the onset of serious deterioration typically occurs quite late in life.

Generally, we reach a peak of physical performance and sensory accomplishment in our 20s. Some aspects of mental performance also peak at around that time while other mental abilities continue to develop throughout most of our adult lives. Muscular strength declines with age, although fitness training can enhance performance at any age. Strength is related to body size and construction, and women are on average physically weaker than men at all ages. Indeed, most men aged 50–80 can be stronger than most women aged 20–30. Figure 4.1 shows, as an example, how much strength people have to twist with two hands – for instance, to open a jam jar. It can be seen that, on average, members of the over-50s age group have less strength than the under-35s, and men are stronger than women for a given age range. But for both age groups the variation between individuals is substantial, and the differences within a group are larger than the differences in average strength between the two groups. This is an illustration of the general situation for physical capabilities, that the variation of performance within an age group is much larger than the variation between the averages for different age groups.

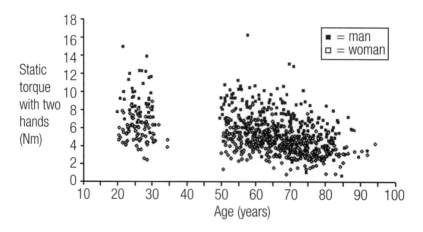

Figure 4.1 Twisting strength using two hands (Reproduced, with permission, from Steenbekkers and van Beijsterveldt, 1998.)

It used to be assumed that physical deterioration was inevitable as people get older. Now it is clear that much of this is due to reduced levels of physical activity, as people take it easy. This means that such deterioration can be halted and reversed through exercise. Older people have the greatest need to maintain their exercise levels, and those with some disease-related impairment may have the most to gain.

Particular aspects of physical performance that decline with age and which are important for functioning include mobility, dexterity and the ability to reach and stretch. Figure 4.2 illustrates how locomotor disability builds up with increasing age. More than a third of people over the age of 75 experience difficulty in getting around.

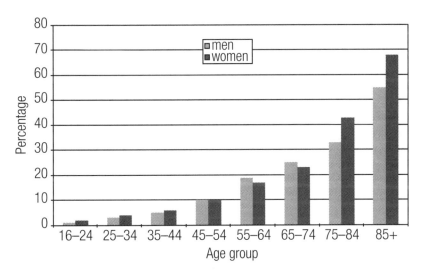

Figure 4.2 Locomotor disability (Data from Bajekal and Prescott, 2003.)

In the case of sensory capabilities, there is a more marked decrease in performance with age, as well as increasing variability between individuals. With advancing age we experience a decline in our ability to see detail, to focus on near objects, to discriminate between levels of contrast, to detect the dimmest of lights, to recover from glare and to adapt to changes in brightness. This is a consequence of changes to the lens and muscles of the eye, which result in long-sightedness and less acute vision. These impairments are helped by spectacles and by environments that use contrast to good effect.

Hearing declines gradually throughout adult life, and is worsened by noisy working environments. The commonest form of hearing loss in older people is reduced sensitivity to sound, particularly at high frequencies. Understanding the spoken word is also affected, especially in the presence of background noise (the problem with drinks parties and pubs). People tend to show less sympathy and more irritation when interacting with someone who is hard of hearing than with those with visual or physical impairment.

Although physical and sensory performance tend to decline with age, variability in this decline is not the dominant source of variability for a population of people over the age of 50. Other sources of variation – genetic and gender – are more important (as indicated in Figure 4.1).

These changes in physical capability with age, and the variability between people, have important implications for the design of products and services used by older people, as is discussed in later chapters. An important characteristic of old age is the occurrence of more than one disability, and indeed of multiple minor disabilities. Any one of these on its own would not be a serious source of difficulty, particularly when taking into account the compensation mechanisms that people devise for themselves. However, a number of such minor disabilities can have an overall impact that may be more than the sum of the parts. This is particularly relevant to complex tasks such as driving.

Mental performance ● ● ● ● ● ● ● ● ● ● ● ●

The potential loss of mental capabilities in later life can be a source of anxiety. This is most likely to be apparent when an individual is faced with a situation that is novel, demanding or complex. In contrast, mental performance based on bodies of information acquired over long periods of time – such as vocabulary, work-related expertise, hobbies and interests – tends to remain comparatively stable with advancing age.

Studies by psychologists in laboratory situations can detect age-related declines in tasks that depend on the speed of mental processing, the degree of attention and concentration, and the ability to do two or more things at a time. Ageing-associated declines are also found in some aspects of language, such as word finding and fluency – the common experience of having words 'on the tip of the tongue' but being unable to articulate them. With advancing age, memory for recent events is more affected than memory for remote events, and recall is more difficult than recognising information when presented.

A useful distinction made by psychologists is between 'crystallised intelligence' and 'fluid intelligence'. *Crystallised intelligence* reflects the amount of knowledge acquired during a lifetime, and shows up as general knowledge, understanding of definitions and concepts, and problem-solving based on existing knowledge. *Fluid intelligence*, on the other hand, is a measure of the ability to solve novel problems; for instance, those for which there are no solutions derivable from education or experience. Crystallised intelligence remains relatively unaffected by ageing but fluid skills begin to decline appreciably in the mid-60s, on average. However, there is considerable individual variation. Variability of test score increases with age for measures of mental performance generally, as we saw earlier for physical performance.

There is some evidence in support of what has been called 'terminal drop' – a rapid decline in mental capabilities in the months before death, following a fairly level performance until that point. The evidence is best for those under the age of 75; for the older old the decline may be more gradual. The gradual decline with age in average mental capabilities seen for populations of older people would then reflect the increase in proportion of the age group approaching death. The onset of chronic conditions such as Alzheimer's disease or depression, the two most prevalent illnesses seen by old-age psychiatrists, of course contributes to the decline in mental performance on the part of those who experience them.

Mental decline with advancing age should not be regarded as a phenomenon totally outside our control. The intuitively persuasive maxim is 'use it or lose it'. There is clear evidence that physical exercise can improve physical performance in later life, as well as aspects of intellectual performance. There is also some evidence for the benefits of mental exercise. Older chess or bridge players are able to play as well as younger players despite quite serious declines in skills such as memory that should be essential to good chess playing. What seems to be happening is that greater experience compensates for loss of more basic skills, although the ability to compensate tends to be less at older ages. The pianist Artur Rubinstein explained how he conquered weaknesses due to ageing in his piano playing by, first, reducing his repertoire and playing a smaller number of pieces, second, practising these pieces more often and, third, by slowing down his speed of playing before fast movements, thereby producing a contrast that enhanced the impression of speed in these fast movements.

Generally, practice and training may boost compensatory mechanisms, rather than affect root skills. Practice continued throughout a lifetime and maintained in old age preserves skills at word finding and recognition. Healthy older people tend to choose activities in which they can retain a high level of function. Factors that help to maintain competence in old age include resolution, optimism, hope, cheerfulness and energy.

The declines in mental performance with age that we have described have been based on studies by psychologists in the laboratory. But some of these findings may simply reflect what researchers can study in the lab. Moreover, under laboratory conditions, age differences show up when people are asked for information that doesn't matter much but not if asked for information that is important to them. In the past few years researchers have developed a much more optimistic view of the ageing mind, influenced in part by the observation that most older people fare quite well in the world. Physiological and cognitive declines measured in the lab don't necessarily map neatly onto everyday life. We now believe that the ageing brain doesn't lose as many nerve cells as was once thought, and that in fact adult brains continue to sprout new cells.

With advancing age it may take longer to pick up new skills. But people retain or even improve their performance in the skills they care about the most. Older people have better social wisdom – for instance, they are able to evaluate a stranger's personality more accurately and have better verbal skills. Despite popular television stereotypes of the cantankerous and whingeing (*One Foot in the Grave*), the evidence is that older people are generally happier than the young, are in better mental health, manage interpersonal relationships more adeptly and suffer fewer negative emotions.

Health and social care ● ● ● ● ● ● ● ● ● ● ●

Life expectancy has been steadily improving, but what about the number of years we can expect to live in good health before age-related disability sets in? The evidence is conflicting, depending on what we mean by 'good health'. If we use as the criterion the ability to perform basic self-care tasks – known as 'activities of daily living' – such as bathing, dressing, getting around, feeding and using the toilet, the evidence suggests that the period during which we become dependent on others for assistance with such tasks has not been increasing as a proportion of our whole life, and indeed may be reducing. On the other hand, using a more subjective criterion – whether people feel that what they can manage is limited by long-standing illness – then there is a lack of evidence of improvement on average over time, despite the objective increase in longevity. One possible explanation is that people have an increasing awareness of ill-health, combined perhaps with improving diagnostic techniques that identify diseases earlier.

The proportion of people reporting a long-standing illness that limits their activities increases with age. Around a quarter of men aged 50–54 report such an illness, rising to almost half of those aged 80 and over. Conversely, self-reported good health declines with age. Over 70 per cent of women in their 50s say their health is good, falling to 50 per cent of those aged 80 and over.

We are increasingly understanding that our ability to age healthily and actively depends on decisions we make about the way we manage our lives. The main things to attend to if we wish to maximise our chances of ageing successfully are a well-balanced diet with plenty of fruit and vegetables, avoiding obesity, not smoking, alcohol in moderation, with regular exercise, mental stimulation and social engagement. Nevertheless, such clean living can only postpone the almost inevitable onset of frailty, when we become increasingly dependent on health care and social care.

The prospect of an ageing population might suggest growing requirements for health and social care for older people and expanding opportunities for businesses to meet those needs. But that would be too simple a conclusion. We are living longer, certainly, and the trend towards increasing longevity seems clear. Life expectancy at the age of 60 has been increasing at the rate of a month or so a year over the past 30 years. But are these extra months a time of ill-health and frailty, added to the existing life course through the efforts of the medical profession to prolong life? Or are they in effect time added to middle age, leaving unchanged the duration of the period of dependency towards life's end? On the whole, the evidence tends to favour the latter viewpoint. For instance, the need for health care falls largely into the last year or so of life, regardless of the age at death, and the amount of health care required by an individual doesn't increase with age at death.

So increasing longevity as such seems unlikely to have much impact on the demand for health care, whether of individuals or of society as a whole. On the other hand, as the baby boom generation grows older, the demand for health and social care will rise, simply because of the larger numbers of that generation. The baby boomers will add about 2 million extra older people to those aged 70 and over in the 2030s – who will amount to some 10 million in total. This implies a significant additional cost of care at that time.

Ageing attitudes ● ● ● ● ● ● ● ● ● ● ● ●

How do our attitudes change as we grow older? Do we get set in our ways, or are we open to new ideas and activities once the drudgery of work has been left behind? Are we forever influenced by the experiences of our youth, or do our attitudes shift as we get older?

Three main factors influence attitudes in later life. First is age itself, because there are psychological changes associated with ageing, as discussed above. Moreover, age is important in determining the stage we are in the life cycle, in particular our experience of major life events such as marriage or loss of spouse. These concrete circumstances are important in shaping attitudes. We may also become more confident as we mature, less easily embarrassed, less bothered by what people might think – the up-side of growing older.

Second, there are the generation effects that relate to the group of people – known as a cohort – with whom we share a year (or, more commonly, a decade) of birth, and with whom we share common experiences, particularly when young, that are different from preceding or succeeding cohorts. The cohort members who were adolescents in the 1950s grew up in a decidedly less permissive climate than did those who were maturing in the 1960s.

Shared experiences within a generation extend beyond attitudes to practical matters that affect lifestyle. For instance, the proportion of women who hold a driving licence increases from one cohort to the next, and the gap between men and women holding a licence narrows in each successive cohort.

Third, there are what is known as period effects – experiences that affect the whole population and permeate all age groups alike: for instance, the development of the consumer society, the expansion of higher education and the growth of work opportunities for women, all in recent decades. One of challenges for social scientists who study ageing is to disentangle age, cohort and period effects when trying to explain how attitudes develop through the life course. Equally, this is a challenge for those attempting to forecast market behaviour.

Some of these influences can be exemplified from studies of how attitudes towards religion, sexual behaviour and welfare expenditure change with age. The proportion of people saying they have no religion declines with age, from 60 per cent of the 18–24 age group to 24 per cent of those aged 65 and over. A similar decline is seen in the beliefs that it is not wrong to have sexual relations before marriage or for adults of the same sex to have a sexual relationship. Tracking successive cohorts over time shows that these attitudes are pretty stable. People do not become more religious with age nor do they change their attitudes to sex. Rather, on these matters each generation acquires its attitudes early on and sticks with them. On the other hand, attitudes across society have become more permissive towards abortion, with each cohort shifting its views.

An example of a life cycle effect can be seen in people's attitudes towards public spending and welfare provision. The priority that people give to health and pension expenditure increases with age, while support for education and child benefit tends to fall.

One new factor affecting attitudes arises from increasing longevity. Those now in their 50s, seeing the prospect of a further 30 years of life, will tend to perceive themselves as 'young', and hence are more likely to engage in active creative leisure pursuits. Older people today commonly feel themselves as 10–15 years younger than they actually are, seeing themselves as middle-aged rather than old. This feeling is of course based on a norm for attitudes and behaviour established by their parents' generation. The actor Jack Nicholson, then aged 61, said: 'I remember what someone of 60 looked like when I was a kid. They didn't look like me.'

A second new effect is the consequence of the growth of educational and employment opportunities in recent decades for women in particular, which will lead to increasing diversity of lifestyles. A third effect is the increase in divorce and remarriage. Whereas in the past the lifestyle of those in their 50s and beyond was characterised by comparative permanence and stability, now there is much greater variation, with the opportunity for both success and failure. Increasing numbers will be living alone, bringing in its wake a greater need to self-manage one's lifestyle (at which women may be more capable than men), and with more people socially isolated and perhaps vulnerable to alcohol and depression. Divorce is bad for men's health as well as for women's wealth.

There has been quite a lot of speculation about the prospects for members of the baby boom generation as they age. (The demographic meaning of the baby boomers was discussed in Chapter 1.) When considering attitudes and expectations, we need to be careful about treating the two post-war baby boom cohorts as identical. The 1946–1950 cohort was born in post-war austerity, rationing and selective education but entered the labour market as the economy was entering a period of prosperity, with opportunities in higher education opening up in the 1960s, together with the availability of the contraceptive pill and the sexual freedom that accompanied it. The second baby boom cohort, of the 1960s, was born into prosperity and comprehensive secondary education but entered working life in the recession of the early 1980s.

Nevertheless, the common experience of both cohorts includes the absence of large-scale military conflict and military service, a cradle-to-grave welfare state, the sexual revolution and the emergence of the consumer society. In all these respects, the experience of the baby boomers is different from that of their parents. Experience conditions attitude. Some analysts argue that two key characteristics of the baby boomers, now and in the future as they get older, are individualism and liberalism. The boomers are more individualistic than their parents, who experienced the collective solidarity of wartime; they are more anti-establishment and non-conformist, less deferential, less trusting of those in authority, less attracted to organised religion. The boomers are the first generation of the age of affluence, who have come to expect individual wants and needs to be satisfied and have been encouraged to define themselves by personal choices.

The baby boomers are more liberal in stance than their parents. The availability of the contraceptive pill and the reform of divorce and abortion laws made a lasting impression on their attitudes and values. This generation has been in the vanguard of the progressive social movements of recent years, including anti-racism, feminism, ethical consumption and the green movement. They tend to take a more liberal line on illegal drugs and are more internationalist in outlook.

These generalisations are based on attitude surveys of the baby boom generation as they are now, and reflect broad tendencies in the responses. There is of course considerable diversity of attitudes, consequent on variations in wealth, education, ethnicity, geography and the like. It should not be assumed that the baby boomers are essentially homogenous, middle class, affluent, monocultural, highly educated, believers in gender equality and the sexual revolution. The present diversity of attitudes is certain to increase as they age. Nevertheless, as the demographic centre of gravity shifts towards higher ages, prevailing attitudes seem likely to become more individualistic and liberal, at least if the baby boomers retain these attitudes acquired in youth as they age.

Work and play ● ● ● ● ● ● ● ● ● ● ● ● ●

The traditional concept of the life course involved 15–20 years of growing and learning, some 40 years of work, followed by perhaps 10 years of retirement. Now, with the extension of education, not to mention gap years and other time off for travel, plus early retirement, we have been thinking increasingly in terms of only 30 years of work followed by perhaps 25 years of rest and play. But this is not financially viable for most people because you cannot put enough current income aside in pension funds and other savings to provide a decent standard of living over such a prolonged period of old age. There has therefore been a reaction against the notion that early retirement – in your 50s – should be the norm, and a greater acceptance that we shall need to go on working for longer. Some argue that the expectation of early retirement for managers and professionals has become entrenched and will be difficult to change. So the 50s age group might polarise between affluent early retirees and those compelled to continue working in low-paid jobs through economic necessity or to get by on invalidity benefit.

Employment among people 50 and over is on the increase, prompted in part by disappointing levels of pensions. In early 2003, 70 per cent of those aged between 50 and state pension age were in employment, which is up from 64 per cent in 1996. Of those over state pension age, 9 per cent are still in work, of whom a quarter are self-employed (they often find it hard to stop). Research suggests that about half of those between 50 and state pension age who are not in employment, as well as 10 per cent of those above pension age, would like remunerated work.

However, it seems probable that the traditional polarisation between work and retirement will become less viable in the future. Some analysts argue that the baby boomers are likely to place greater value on the work–life balance and hence to seek flexibility in late working life, developing a diverse portfolio of careers (including moonlighting while still in full-time employment) that reflects their increasing experience of part-time work and self-employment during their main career.

As full-time work ends or is phased down, and as family-raising responsibilities come to an end, so does the time available for leisure increase. It is therefore surprising that for most of the present generation over retirement age there is a decrease in time spent on leisure pursuits, or at best a similar amount, compared with people in younger age groups. This is perhaps less unexpected for sports and physical activities, where health and mobility problems increase with age. Surveys find that walking is by far the predominant activity reported in surveys of older people, half the men in their 60s and 40 per cent of women reporting this. Cycling, snooker, golf, swimming and bowls were activities reported by more than 5 per cent of men aged 60–69, and swimming and keep-fit by women. Television is the ubiquitous home-based leisure activity, the hours watched increasing with age. The average duration of television watching is 25 hours per week for the whole population, 29 hours for the age group 55–64 and 36 hours for the over-65s. Radio, listening to music, reading, gardening, and visiting friends and relatives are reported by over half of men and women aged 60–69, with DIY important for men and dressmaking/

needlework/knitting important for women. Among the away-from-home cultural events, cinema shows a clear decline with age, while attendance at classical music performances, art galleries and exhibitions hold up well until the age of 70. Older people are more likely to belong to a religion and to attend services than those in the younger age groups.

But this is the present picture – how the present generation of older people spend their leisure time. We may be confident that subsequent generations will be more active, and active for longer, reflecting improving health and more positive attitudes. But the pattern of activities will surely change, with for example a likely decline in involvement with religion.

Living arrangements

Family life changes over time, and the proportion of people who are married declines with advancing age, mostly because husbands die before their wives – a consequence of shorter life expectancy for men and the fact that women tend to marry men older than themselves. Around 80 per cent of men aged 60–69 are married but only 65 per cent of women; for the age group 70–79 the figures are about 70 per cent and 40 per cent respectively. The numbers of older divorced people and those cohabiting are on the increase, reflecting the ageing of the generation that experienced increasing divorce rates in the 1970s and after.

Marital status of course has a strong effect on household composition. There has been an increase over the years in the proportion of older people living alone or with their spouse only, and a corresponding fall in the proportion living in family households. Half of all women aged 65 and over live alone, but only a quarter of all men.

The majority of older people are now owner-occupiers, over half of those over 60 owning outright and some 10 per cent still paying off a mortgage. About a third rent their housing, mostly from local authorities and housing associations. Eighty per cent of those over 50 live in houses, and only 20 per cent in flats. As people get older, dependency tends to increase, and sheltered housing of one kind or another becomes an option. Around 10 per cent of people aged 75 and over live in sheltered housing.

Conclusions ● ● ● ● ● ● ● ● ● ● ● ● ● ●

So what, after all this, is it like to be old? Most older people have little discernible impairment. Typically, those in reasonable health report feeling just like they felt before they became old, except not being able to do certain things, and with an awareness of their bodies as sources of some slight malaise, often forgettable but always there if thought about.

But, however actively, healthily and successfully we plan to age, disability, frailty and death eventually catch up with us. Nevertheless, the timing is not predetermined. We can undoubtedly delay the onset of decrepitude by adopting a healthy and active lifestyle through the course of our adult lives, and indeed there are benefits in clean living however late we might start. Partly through recognition of the virtues of active ageing, older people today are fitter, stronger and more capable than those in the past.

Because our capabilities relate to how actively we use them, differences between individuals of the same age are far greater than average differences between age groups. Yet at the same time, age is a great equaliser; class differences in health and well-being become less marked as later life progresses.

What, then, is the significance of 'being old' before the onset of late life disability? Well, we clock up birthdays and reach symbolic ages such as 60 when we are entitled to concessionary fares on the buses, then the state pension age, and later milestones as the decades pass, culminating in the greeting from the Queen for those who reach a century not out. In our society, chronological age has a powerful resonance. It conditions people's expectations: 'doing well for her age', as they say, or 'he's showing his age'. But these expectations are becoming dated as longevity increases. So now we proclaim, with some reason, that '60 is the new 50' and the like. The factor linked to chronological age that is slowest to change is the age of pension entitlement, though even here we are beginning to see upward movement. For instance, the state pension age for women is being raised to 65, with phasing in over the period 2010 to 2020.

Chronological age is certainly a rough proxy for the cumulative impact of 'life' on an individual. But a better measure of our physical and mental state is how far one is away from the end of life, rather than how far from the beginning. For the majority of us who escape both sudden death from acute disease and the chronic degenerative conditions of later life, such as Alzheimer's, frailty and the need for care are mostly confined to a relatively compressed year or two in the run-up to death, regardless of the age at which we might die. Until then, most of us can expect to remain in passable health, with luck.

Nevertheless, being old is undoubtedly a distinct life stage in that one has experienced youth and middle age, might have been married to one person for half a lifetime, might have brought up children to adulthood, and in the process have acquired considerable experience, not to say wisdom. There is also the inevitable experience of loss. A fifth of women have lost their husbands by the age of 65, over a third by 75, and about half of the present over-65s are likely to be dead ten years from now. Whilst some of our attitudes reflect this changing perspective, others remain largely unchanged from youth – hence the common feeling that what is odd about growing old is that you don't feel any different.

Perhaps the main contemporary tensions are between optimism and pessimism in later life. Between the desire of the optimists to age successfully and the inevitable onset of frailty, dependency and loss of accustomed autonomy. Between the optimism of those planning to take full advantage of a financially well-provided for old age and the pessimism of those who do not perceive their later life prospects as at all rosy. And between the optimism of those who actively seek to prevent the onset of disability in later life by adopting a healthy lifestyle and those not persuaded that the effort involved is worthwhile, given their expectation of poor health and quality for the remainder of their lives.

What, then, are the implications of this chapter for businesses thinking about the implications of an ageing population? Two main points to make:

- As always, get closer to your customers – in this case your older customers. Talk to them, mix with them, recognise their diversity, understand their wants and needs. If you're not of their age group yourself, operate across generational boundaries – inter-generationally. Look out for differences between successive generations. Avoid stereotypes and simplifications. Tap into the research literature, talk to those who study ageing, commission market research.

- Think how you could help your mature customers with the things that matter most to them: maintaining good health and physical functioning, freedom from depression, personal optimism, well-retained mental abilities, engaging in social activities, feeling supported, living in a good, safe neighbourhood.

Further reading

Bajekal, M. and Prescott, A. (2003) 'Disability', in *Health Survey for England 2001*. London: The Stationery Office

Bassey, E.J. (1997) 'Physical capabilities, exercise and ageing'. *Reviews in Clinical Gerontology*, vol 7, pages 289–297

Evandrou, M. (ed). (1997) *Baby Boomers: ageing in the 21st century*. London: Age Concern England

Harkin, J. and Huber, J. (2004) *Eternal Youths*. London: Demos

Helmuth, L. (2003) 'The wisdom of the wizened', *Science*, vol 299, pages 1300–1302

Huber, J. and Skidmore, P. (2003) *The New Old: why the baby boomers won't be pensioned off*. London: Demos

Huppert, F. (2003) 'Designing for older users', in: Clarkson, J., Coleman, R., Keates, S. and Lebbon, C. (eds). (2003) *Inclusive Design: design for the whole population*. London: Springer-Verlag

Marmot, M., Banks, J., Blundell, R., et al (eds). (2003) *Health, Wealth and Lifestyles of the Older Population in England: the 2002 English Longitudinal Study of Ageing*. London: Institute of Fiscal Studies

Matheson, J. and Summerfield, C. (eds). (1999) *Social Focus on Older People*. London: Office for National Statistics/The Stationery Office

Park, A. (2000) 'The generation game', in: *British Social Attitudes 17th report*. London: National Centre for Social Research/Sage

Rowe, J. and Kahn, R. (1999) *Successful Aging*. New York: Dell Publishing

Scales, J. and Scase, R. (2000) *Fit and Fifty?* Swindon: Economic and Social Research Council

Steenbekkers, L. and van Beijsterveldt, C. (eds). (1998) *Design-relevant Characteristics of Ageing Users*. Delft: Delft University Press

Stuart-Hamilton, I. (2000) *The Psychology of Ageing*, 3rd edition. London: Jessica Kingsley

Traynor, J. and Walker, A. (2003) *People Aged 65 and Over*. London: Office of National Statistics/The Stationery Office

Worcester, R. (1999) *Grey Power: the changing face*. London: Help the Aged

5 : Market segmentation

In the previous chapter we saw how large and diverse is the group of people on whom our attention is focused. We are dealing with 20 million people currently over the age of 50, a figure projected to grow to 25 million by 2020, when they will comprise half the adult population. Their range of interests is exceptionally wide and encompasses most of the interests of younger generations. Grandparents are as much in the market for toys and children's clothes as are parents. The over-50s are major users of leisure services of all kinds.

Given the magnitude and variability of people over 50, it makes little sense to think of marketing to this age group as a whole. It is necessary to segment this market into manageable sub-groups that share similar characteristics. For each such sub-group, marketing messages need to have a high resonance and be directed via the most effective media, and marketing packages must be economically viable. A sub-group should be one that its members feel comfortable to be part of – the group should recognise itself.

The difficulty is to decide how best to segment the mature market. A number of approaches are advocated. We review the main possibilities below.

Age

It is conventional in market analysis to segment primarily by age, with socio-economic status providing finer detail, and to focus on age groups in the range 20–50, with 50+ lumped in one box. A slightly less crude approach is to split the over-50s into two groups: 50–64 and 65+.

For businesses that wish to focus on the mature market, a natural development is to refine the age segments; for instance, into the 'young old' (age range 55–64), 'middle old' (65–74) and 'old old' (75 and over).

Other versions of age-based segmentation that are advocated by one expert or another include:

- 3 segments: thrivers (50–60), seniors (60–70), elders (70–80+).

- 4 segments: pre-retirement (late 50s), retirement (60–69), long retired (70–84), advanced age (85+).

- 5 segments: early mature years (50–54); full bloomers (55–59); pre-retirees (60–64), prime retirees (65–75), seniors (76+).

The main attraction of age-based segmentation is that it is straightforward to achieve. We live in a society in which everyone who is of sound mind knows their age (indeed, knowing your age is a requirement for being judged compos mentis). And, clearly, there is a general relation between age and the onset of age-related impairments of health that, sooner or later, catch up with us in later life. However, the correlation between age and behaviour is by no means straightforward.

Counting the years from birth is not a particularly good indication of a person's health status or any other important characteristic. (As discussed in Chapter 4, counting the years to death is much more relevant, although not in practice possible in a marketing context, of course.) Far more variety is found in a randomly selected group of 70-year-olds than in a group of 30-year-olds. The former could include people still playing competitive sports at senior level, as well as the frail; those productively employed and those fully retired; those who are fully engaged in their communities and those who are reclusive; those open to new products and services and those who are conservative in their buying habits. So chronological age, while easy to ascertain, is not a straightforward guide to the characteristics likely to be of interest to those offering goods and services to the mature market.

There is, however, a link between age and the attitudes that people hold, as discussed in Chapter 4. Age is a determinant of where people are in their life cycle, the experience they share with others in their cohort, as well as the changes over their lifetime that have affected the whole population. The experience for men of compulsory military service in the 1950s was very different from that of having been young in the 1960s, experiences that are likely to form attitudes, values and preferences that persist in later life and influence marketplace behaviour. Such thinking is the basis of what is known as 'generational marketing', where the emphasis is on the defining characteristics of successive cohorts.

There are two, perhaps three, situations where age-based segmentation seems particularly appropriate. The first is for financial services linked to retirement determined by age (although the prevalence of early retirement makes the link to a specific birthday less clear-cut than it once was). The second is where common shared attitudes form the basis for the marketing approach; for instance, for collectible display items or 'golden oldie' CDs that reflect nostalgia for a rose-tinted youth. And perhaps a third, for dating agency services, where chronological age seems to be an important criterion for those participating. The magazine of the AARP (formerly known by its full name, the American Association of Retired Persons) offers online dating assistance to its over-50s readers, and in Britain some Internet-based dating services do not employ any upper age limit.

Those who are keen on aged-based segmentation will generally paint pen pictures of each generation. For the 60–70 age group, for instance, we might be told that this is the cohort for whom the term 'teenager' was first coined. They were children during post-war austerity, who grew up as the consumer boom gathered momentum in the 1950s, and were in their 20s during the social revolution of the 1960s. They are still enjoying life, are more affluent than previous generations, better educated, more widely travelled, and are redefining what it means to be 'old' in Britain today.

Such a pen picture is undoubtedly evocative of some shared experience. Much of the commercial interest in the ageing baby boomers is based on the supposition that their distinctive attitudes, formed when young and shared through adult life, will facilitate a targeted approach to marketing when they are older and wealthier. This is not implausible. Nevertheless, we must recall our regular proviso that generalisations about large groups need to be treated with caution, given the diversity of those who comprise that group. They may all be members of the same cohort, but they'll vary hugely, and large minorities will not share the attitudes or do the things supposedly characteristic of that generation. Beware of stereotyping.

There is also the important question of which attitudes we retain as we grow older, which we discard and which new ones we acquire. We could be more confident in predicting the attitudes of the baby boomers in later life if we were able to rely on proven principles concerning attitudinal change and stability. What we actually know is quite limited, because of the not inconsiderable research task involved in following a representative group over long periods of time. So we tend to seize upon straws in the wind to get a sense of what's happening – imagining, for instance, that the growth in popularity of 'green funerals' and woodland burials reflects significant changes in attitudes both to the environment and to conventional behaviour.

Age is the most obvious basis for segmenting older people into conceptually manageable categories. It is easy to do but big questions remain about its usefulness in generating targets for effective marketing.

Income

Income is of course highly relevant to consumption patterns. As we saw in Chapter 2, there is no great change in income or expenditure around retirement. A reduction in both by some 20 per cent on average following retirement reflects lower income offset by fewer financial obligations. In terms of purchasing power, new pensioners are therefore in a pretty similar position financially to late-working-age people of similar socio-economic status. They are no more likely to be poor than their somewhat younger counterparts. The range of incomes in later life is nearly as broad as for working life. (However, as discussed in Chapter 2, expenditure patterns show some differences.)

Older people, on average, continue to save throughout retirement, accumulating substantial net financial wealth as well as housing wealth. As noted in Chapter 2, the financial net wealth of those over 50 is over £500 billion. It would seem a reasonable assumption that net financial wealth and income will generally run in parallel. (On the other hand, housing wealth and income do not necessarily go hand in hand, as some low-income owner-occupiers may have substantial housing assets.)

Given this position, segmentation of the mature market by socio-economic category would be natural. A basic split may be made between the more up-market ABC1s and the down-market C2DEs. More refined segmentations may be justifiable. For instance, Robert Diamond suggests that, as children leave home and the mortgage gets paid off, financial commitments may fall faster than disposable income through the retirement transition, opening up a degree of 'financial freedom', which will vary from individual to individual. He links three degrees of financial freedom (high, medium, low) to a two-fold independence/dependence dichotomy, to yield a six-category segmentation based on income and health.

Education must also be a significant factor in determining the purchasing behaviour of older consumers. There is a lack of hard information but a reasonable supposition is that educational attainment will track socio-economic status for any given generation, while increasing of course from one generation to the next.

Life stages

The life course begins with birth and ends with death, and in between we recognise a series of stages through which we move. Shakespeare's seven ages of man are still those we recognise, including the sixth age of the 'lean and slipper'd pantaloon with spectacles on nose', and the final stage of 'second childishness and mere oblivion, sans teeth, sans eyes, sans taste, sans everything'. More relevant to our present discussion is the fifth stage mature consumer, 'in fair round belly with good capon lin'd'.

The life stages comprising 'later life' span many more years than those for youth. For the purposes of sub-dividing the over-50s, we need to identify distinguishing features more subtle than the simple split into the active Third Agers and the frail Fourth Agers. Life stages are related to age, of course, but are not defined by age. Indeed, with growing longevity, and the prospects of extended healthy ageing, chronological age bands seem increasingly out of place.

The kinds of characteristics that might be used to define a life stage include:

- health status, particularly the onset of chronic disease or disability;

- mobility, reflecting both health status and social orientation;

- family responsibilities – children having flown the nest, yet perhaps with the need still to care for long-lived parents;

- financial status – outgoings decreased as mortgages paid off and children no longer dependent, and non-employed so no longer at risk of unemployment;

- major 'life events', such as loss of a spouse whether through divorce or death, or, for some, becoming a grandparent.

Evidently, there are quite a number of characteristics that could be used to delineate discrete life stages that might form the basis of potentially useful segmentation. There is a tension here between *lumping* characteristics together to retain a simple overall categorisation and *splitting* to generate a more refined yet more complicated typology.

Perhaps the simplest approach is exemplified by the National Service Framework for Older People, the National Health Service guide to meeting the health needs of the older population. This involves just three life episodes defined by health status:

- Entering old age – completed career in paid employment and/or child rearing but still active and independent.

- Transitional, between healthy active life and frailty, which often occurs in the seventh or eighth decades.

- Frail old age, often experienced only late in life.

A slightly more elaborate formulation has been developed by George Moschis, a marketing academic at the Center for Mature Consumer Studies, Georgia State University. He recognises both health status and life events, and the interaction between the two, in a four-fold categorisation:

- 'Healthy indulgers', who behave largely like younger consumers.

- 'Ailing outgoers', who experience a chronic disease or disability, so are concerned about their health, but retain positive self-esteem. They constitute a prime market for consumer products and services to meet their needs, including health foods, functional clothing and assistive technologies, although lack of mobility may limit consumption and affect lifestyle.

- 'Healthy hermits' have experienced an adverse life event, such as the death of a spouse, which has triggered social withdrawal. They tend to have few consumption-related needs and to be negative towards innovation.

- 'Frail recluses', who are experiencing both biological and social ageing and who may need support in day-to-day needs, whether in their own homes or in residential care.

These four life stages are not envisaged as being on a simple linear pathway. Rather, the path diverges according to whether health deteriorates before or after an adverse life event – see Figure 5.1. In the former case, the initial outcome is to become an ailing outgoer; in the latter case, a healthy hermit. When both have happened, you become a frail recluse, according to Moschis's scheme. An important feature of this and other such approaches is that chronological age is not employed to delineate life stages.

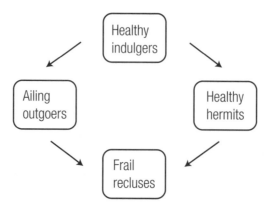

Figure 5.1 Moschis's four life stages

The healthy hermit category points to the possibility of using living alone, or not, as a basis for segmentation. Living alone is easy to define, increases with age and is a category for which considerable data exist, as discussed in previous chapters. Needs and wants vary, depending on whether older people live singly or in couples – for instance, for communications, social engagement, single-portion prepared food, home help and indeed for pre-arranged funerals which are common in other countries such as the Netherlands and Spain though not in the UK.

The ailing outgoers respond to offers that meet their particular needs; for instance, that of older women suffering from arthritis for functional clothing allowing ease of dressing and undressing and for movement, or for home modifications that facilitate independent living. Frail recluses are in the market for domiciliary services tailored to their individual needs.

Another approach to life stage segmentation is based on a study of affluent people in the age range 45–65, conducted by Kath Harris. This pointed to a majority group of retired (or semi-retired) 'empty nesters', enjoying family life stability and an enviable lifestyle – what has been termed the 'the long vacation'. This group contrasts with two others: those still with children at home, for whom this was a preoccupation; and those still in work, who also may be less satisfied with their lives.

A problem with such relatively simple schemes of segmentation based on life stages is the way that changing lifestyles have complicated the traditional flows of the past, as discussed next.

Lifestyle ● ● ● ● ● ● ● ● ● ● ● ● ● ● ●

As life expectancy has increased and retirement has come earlier, the length of the Third Age has grown. Incomes in later life have risen and educational attainment is increasing, as well as career opportunities, particularly for women. Divorce and remarriage are becoming more common, as are second families, late families, active singles in their 50s and 60s – these don't fit easily into a life stage approach. All this is opening up a wider range of lifestyles for older people. So we may be seeing a rejection of the conventional life stage cycle brought on by the ageing process. Chosen lifestyle may be more meaningful as a basis for segmentation than position in the life cycle.

Compared with the young, older people have more time – are 'time-rich' – and so have more opportunities for holidays and leisure activities such as gardening and television watching, and more time for civic and voluntary activity. They may feel wiser, more settled and confident in their views; less likely perhaps to experience embarrassment; more individualistic and less influenced by the unifying culture of global media and technology.

Compared with previous generations of older people, a greater proportion of the present cohort seems to be adopting a more positive, optimistic, individualistic stance, buying into ideas of healthy, successful, active ageing. They aim to lead independent rewarding lifestyles as long as possible. With this goes, to some degree, a denial of ageing, reflected in a widespread wish to maintain youthful appearances, the attitude that '60 is the new 50', and a corresponding boldness in undertaking adventurous activities and travel destinations (often the kinds of trips usually associated with gap year students). More self-confidence results in their being more demanding about the quality of goods and services.

The main determinants of lifestyle in later life are health, independence and self-sufficiency. Time is also relevant, and indeed lifestyles are shaped partly by whether consumers are constrained by time or by money. Philip Kotler cites the example of one US supermarket chain that successfully reorganised its self-service meat cabinets not by type of meat (beef, pork etc) but by lifestyle, such as meals in minutes and meat for those who like to cook. Such segmentation cuts across life stages.

One particular kind of lifestyle segmentation, developed by Millennium Direct, a company specialising in the mature market, identifies four groups:

- 'recent retirees' with lump sums and new routines, time and money at their disposal for the first time;

- 'solid singles', displaying consistent participation in social and sporting events, perhaps to maintain social contact;

- 'self-starters' who had been self-employed, generally more active than others in finance, current affairs, theatre, art, computers; and

- 'artificial affluents', a newly emerging segment using money from equity release to enjoy a better quality retirement.

Another approach to segmentation that generates sub-groups related to lifestyle is that developed by the communications agency ODM UK, which surveyed 1,700 consumers in the age range 45–89 years, asking a battery of questions about attitudes. The responses were analysed within a framework comprising two dimensions: positive/negative outlook on life, and positive/negative attitude to new things (whether technology, brands or experiences). Seven clusters of respondents emerged from this analysis. For instance, the so-called *live wires* had a positive outlook and were positive about innovation; the *nostalgia seekers* were negative about both, while the *happy and fulfilled* were positive in attitude but only mildly in favour of novelty. Detailed interviews and diary keeping with samples from each segment allowed a fuller picture to be developed of behavioural characteristics, including brand loyalty and use of media. One conclusion drawn is that age is becoming increasingly irrelevant as a targeting tool, because people of the same age can have widely different approaches to life. From this perspective, attitude to life has driven their destinies and will continue to shape the different paths they take.

Segmentation – the bottom line ● ● ● ● ● ● ● ●

What we are seeking are strong explanations for consumer behaviour. In practice, we usually have to be content with weak explanations. This is because of the complexity of the factors that influence such behaviour, particularly that of mature consumers.

Philip Kotler, author of a popular textbook, argues that, to be useful, market segments must be:

- measurable – size, purchasing power, characteristics;

- substantial – big enough to justify the effort of targeting;

- accessible – they can be reached and served;

- differentiable – they respond differently to different marketing mixes;

- actionable.

This constitutes a helpful checklist to assess any proposed segmentation scheme for the mature market.

The mature market is large and diverse, so segmentation into a manageable number of sub-categories is unavoidable. The purpose of attempting to segment mature consumers into discrete categories is to allow marketing effort to be focused cost-effectively. So it is not enough for a segmentation scheme to appear reasonable, based on conceptual thinking or the analysis of market research data. It is necessary to show that segments respond differently to marketing offerings because they reflect differences in underlying values and motivations of the different classes of consumer. Validation of a proposed scheme of segmentation is difficult. Market research usually looks at purchase intentions rather than actual purchases.

An important question is whether segmentation of the mature market is best based on general approaches such as those discussed in previous sections or should be closely tied to the specific product or service in question, as some experts argue. So, for instance, to segment the market for cruises, it may be best to research attitudes towards cruises and destinations. More generally, there seems to be a good case to start with a generic segmentation based on factors such as age, income, life stage or lifestyle. Then a product-specific sub-segmentation might be developed, based on attitudes and behaviour that would be particularly relevant to the product or service – for instance, personality factors such as feelings about innovation.

How should the choice be made between the different generic approaches to segmentation discussed earlier? Marketing students are taught the value of segmentation by customer benefits rather than by product features. From this perspective, age-based segmentation is relevant for financial services, where the timing of the transition to retirement is linked to age (although less precisely than in the past), and also for marketing things with 'retro' appeal. Segmentation by income is pertinent to the marketing of luxury goods and high-value services, where older consumers comprise a dominant market element. Segmentation by life stage is most germane to the marketing of goods and services that slow the transition to frailty by countering physical deterioration (nutrient supplements and exercise, for instance), and promoting independence and autonomy (home aids and adaptations, for example). Lifestyle segmentation is particularly relevant for leisure activities, holidays and travel, where the service offered can respond to the positive attributes of individuals, their elective choices as opposed their unavoidable needs.

There is some scope for combining these generic approaches, in particular to segment by both income and one of the other approaches, to target customers for the higher value end of a range of products and services.

There is no off-the-shelf solution for segmenting the mature market. Each company has to work out the best approach for its product lines based on the characteristics of its customer base and its own business priorities. Segmentation needs to be based on insights into the 'what and why' of customer behaviour. This is particularly challenging in the mature market, the least well understood of all the market sectors.

A successful marketing campaign will boost revenues and profits from the chosen segments. But such success depends on all of the links in the chain contributing – product design, manufacture, supply logistics, pricing, advertising, point of sale marketing and the rest. Partly, no doubt, for reasons of commercial confidentiality, there is a dearth of publicly available business case studies of successful marketing campaigns directed to segments of the mature market. Those who attend the worthwhile marketing conferences dedicated to the over-50s market can certainly learn about what appear to be well-conceived campaigns, but the bottom line success is not generally spelled out, whether on account of commercial confidentiality or because of lack of such success. Nevertheless, useful nuggets can be gained from such events.

In many fields of endeavour what is known as the '80–20' rule is held to apply, meaning that 80 per cent of the benefit of a portfolio of projects is derived from 20 per cent of the projects constituting the portfolio. The other 80 per cent of project are loss making or at best break even. It would not be surprising if marketing to mature consumers worked in this way, so that genuinely successful campaigns would comprise a minority of the total of those undertaken, details of which would be closely guarded on that account.

Academic researchers based in marketing departments of business schools contribute ideas and some research data relevant to the question of how best to segment the mature market. Generally, it seems that the mature market is among the least researched and understood of marketing segments, with many unsupported statements and myths. Academic commentators have questioned the explanatory power for consumer behaviour of demographic and lifestyle factors as well as life stage segmentation. However, what is not clear is whether much can usefully be said in general terms about the benefits of particular approaches to market segmentation; or whether the best approach depends on the particular product or service under consideration. For instance, a statement by an experienced marketing professional that, for his sector, segmentation is most successful when based on product differentiation, may or may not apply more generally. We don't know because the evidence is not available (or at least hard to come by).

Those in the marketing business have their preferred approaches to segmentation, sometimes based on proprietary research techniques. How one might seek to benefit from such expertise is considered in Chapter 9.

Further reading

Diamond, R. (2003) 'Unlocking the value of the over-50 consumer', *Admap*, May, pages 30–33

Harris, K. (2000) 'Silver service: what drives the greying market?', *Admap*, November, pages 33–36

Help the Aged. (2002) *Marketing and Advertising to Older People*, Report of a seminar held on 19 September 2002. London: Help the Aged

Kotler, P. (2003) *Marketing Management*, 11th edition (especially Chapter 10). London: Prentice Hall

Lavery, K. (ed). (1999) *The Definitive Guide to Mature Advertising and Marketing*. Shipley: Millennium Direct

Morgan, C. and Levy, D. (2002) 'The boomer attitude', *American Demographics*, October

Moschis, G. (1996) *Gerontographics*. Westport CT: Quorum Books

Moschis, G. (1996) 'Life stages of the mature market', *American Demographics*, September

OMD UK. (2004) *Understanding Fifties and Over*. London: OMD (UK)

Walker Smith, J. and Clurman, A. (1997) *Rocking the Ages: the Yankelovich report on generational marketing*. New York: HarperBusiness

Worcester, R. (1999) *Grey Power: the changing face*. London: Help the Aged

6 Mainstream markets

In Chapter 2 we showed that older people have many similar needs to the rest of the population. Unless they are living in a care home, all older people still need to purchase many of the same kinds of articles as those purchased by everyone else. They buy food, clothes, kitchen utensils, household items, cars, holidays, financial products etc. One way suppliers can capitalise on the increasing numbers of older people in the population is to ensure that their mainstream products and services are readily usable by those older people. This brings us to the concept of 'inclusive design' with which most of this chapter is concerned – the design of products and services to be usable by as large a proportion of the population as is economically viable. We also look at the emerging practice of mass customisation – the ability to produce customised products at mass market prices as a way of delivering inclusively designed products and services.

Inclusive design – the consumers' case

Many older people have one or more impairments to their physical, sensory or cognitive capabilities, brought about by the natural consequences of the ageing process. This may mean that they can no longer easily use everyday products designed for the majority of the population. As both the absolute and the relative numbers of older people increase, manufacturers and providers of mainstream products and services whose offerings fail to meet the needs of older people will risk losing market share. In this chapter we consider primarily the comparatively large number of older people with single or multiple minor impairments – not those with major impairments, whose needs are considered more in the next chapter. As we saw earlier, the main impairments of old age are progressive reductions in strength, manual dexterity, flexibility and reach, mobility, and impairment of hearing and sight, all of which may impinge on an individual's ability to use a particular product. In addition, there are those with cognitive impairments, such as a loss of memory or difficulty in concentrating for long periods, who find it harder to comprehend and remember complex instructions, thereby rendering the associated products difficult to use.

The design of most everyday products makes assumptions about the normal range of characteristics of the potential users. Much use has been made of a set of standard anthropometric measures (height, weight, reach, etc) that enable the 'one size fits all' philosophy that is necessary for the mass production of goods at low prices. This focus on the majority means that the minority of people, whose characteristics fall outside the 90–95 per cent limits commonly used, find that they are unable to buy or use products that meet their needs. Increasingly, however, the view is being taken that disability is a function of the environment, not of the individual – the so-called *social model of disability*. In other words, it is not the user's fault if they cannot use something; it is the provider of the product or service who is at fault.

The World Health Organization (WHO) makes the important distinction between impairment, disability and handicap. An older person may suffer an impairment, for instance poor eyesight caused by the ageing process. If the impairment is beyond the reach of medical cure, they find themselves disabled in (most) situations where the ability to see is important. As a consequence of this disability, they would then suffer a handicap compared with other people, for example being unable to work or travel. On the other hand, a person with no vision at all would not be disabled in a darkened room (because of the lack of light), and would not therefore be at a handicap compared with people with normal vision. Indeed, it is probably the people with normal sight who would be handicapped in these circumstances.

This change in concept of disability in the last 20 years, away from being primarily a medical concern towards one that focuses on the role of individuals in society, has led to a reconsideration in the design of products that can be used by people generally, with or without impairments. In particular, this has led to the concept of *inclusive design*: design that does not exclude people because of the design features of the product itself. The fundamental concept underlying inclusive design is that all products should be designed to be usable by as broad a range of users as possible. It means taking account of the needs of people with a range of impairments wherever practical, minimising the number of people who have to purchase a specialist product. Thus a telephone with large buttons that also contains an inductive loop mechanism for those with hearing aids is going to be attractive to more people than one that does not. In marketing terms, this means it is likely to have a larger available market – the proportion of the total market for which a product is suitable in terms of functionality and usability.

Note that a fundamental aspect of the inclusive approach is to expand the target group of a product or service to include as many users as possible, without compromising the business goals of return on investment and customer satisfaction. This pragmatic view of the inclusive design approach clearly recognises the need to balance social and commercial pressures. In practice, inclusively designed products meet the needs of a wide range of users through one of three mechanisms:

1. The product can be used directly with no degree of adaptation required by the user or of the product; for example, fitting domestic appliances with controls that can easily be operated by people with arthritic hands or a weak grip. Many aspects of design such as these may involve either little or no extra manufacturing cost, just some extra thought in the design process.

2. Customising the product to a user's needs by modifying its characteristics; for example, increasing the font size of visual displays. At present, this customisation is usually done by the users. In future, information held on a smart card inserted by

the user could effect the customisation automatically. Standards are already in place regarding the coding and use of such information.

3. Provision of interfaces to the product so that a specialist device could be attached to the product; for instance, a specialised keyboard.

Microsoft, for example, adopts options 2 and 3 in the incorporation of the accessibility features built into its Windows operating systems and applications software, without compromising usability for other users. It is not unknown for many users to find that the accessibility features contain useful functionality for their circumstances. An independent report commissioned by Microsoft showed that up to 57 per cent of the (US) population could benefit from the accessibility features, because of minor impairments.

Whilst inclusive design is primarily a UK term, there are similar terms in use throughout the world, such as universal design, barrier-free design, accessible design and design for all. In the USA, a multi-disciplinary team of architects, product designers, engineers and environmental design researchers has published a set of universal design guidelines for use in a wide range of design disciplines, including the built environment, consumer products and communications systems. These guidelines can be applied to the audit of products as well as to their design. The European term is 'Design for All', although it should be noted that there is no intent here to encourage the design of products that suit literally everyone. This would be economically impossible.

It would be a mistake to think that inclusive design benefits only older people or people with disabilities. Designing for people with impairments often brings benefits to other users, including those who are temporarily disabled (eg through injury or illness, pregnancy, with pram/children, carrying shopping) or disabled by the environment (we can all be blinded by a low sun, causing glare and reflections we cannot avoid). For example, low-loading buses are also easier for everyone to get on and off, reducing the time that buses need to spend at the bus stops. 'Pensioner' shopping trolleys in supermarkets (designed to avoid the need for reaching down to get the contents at the bottom) are also easier for people with small amounts of shopping and have proved popular with shoppers of all ages.

Many studies have found that older people neither need nor want specially designed products. They want to be treated like everyone else and to be able to buy what other people buy. Specially designed products are likely to be more expensive and are increasingly seen as stigmatising by those who have to use them – nobody likes to think of themself as old or disabled. As St Augustine suggested in the fourth century AD, 'you only grow old on the outside'. Unfortunately, the outside is what other people see first; the secret of successful design lies in seeing deeper.

Inclusive design – the business case

Over the past 20 years, an extensive body of research literature has been developed, particularly in software engineering, concerned with user-centred design. A major part of this has been the development of methods and tools for involving users directly in the design process, to identify their real needs, to measure their performance in carrying out tasks, etc. This has proved necessary because of our inability to predict how people will interact with complex products. In many areas of engineering science there are good theoretical models that can be used at the design stage to predict how the final system will work; for instance, in civil engineering and electrical power generation. In other areas a more empirical approach has to be followed. A particular issue in the design of complex products involving software is that a designer's view of how the product should be used is not necessarily the same as that of the end-user. This mismatch is frequently a major cause of why products are unusable.

This user-centred approach is an essential underpinning of inclusive design that now has a growing research literature of its own. As yet there are very few published case studies showing the commercial benefits of inclusively designed products. This compares poorly with the large body of published software engineering research showing the benefits of adopting a user-centred approach to the design of IT products and services. However, there is some evidence that commercial organisations are beginning to find that the application of an inclusive design approach removes the need to provide additional or special services for small numbers of less-able-bodied people. More evidence is likely to be forthcoming as many organisations find that they have to meet the requirements of the Disability Discrimination Act 1995 (DDA) with regard to publicly offered services.

Throughout the world, industry seems insensitive to or unaware of the needs of older customers, despite the publicity an ageing population has received over a number of years. A recent survey by the EU-funded SENIORWATCH project revealed that, of the 10,000 senior (over the age of 50) Europeans interviewed, nearly 50 per cent thought their interests in adequate design were not considered by manufacturers of IT products, and more than 70 per cent perceived the media as associating these technologies only with young people. This is consistent with an earlier Design Council study that found that only about a third of the UK FTSE 100 companies were aware of older users. Similar attitudes are reported from the USA.

In developing the business case, we have mapped the arguments for inclusive design onto a framework of seven generic business drivers:

- legislation
- standards
- procurement
- competitive threat
- customer feedback
- competitive advantage
- brand.

Here we look at some of the more important business arguments from this framework.

Legislation

Legislation is undoubtedly a very persuasive form of business driver. However, it is not the legislation itself that provides the drive; it is the prospect of expensive and public litigation arising from failing to meet the requirements of the legislation. The USA has the strongest legislative climate, both with regard to the design and supply of accessible products and in the willingness of people to sue for non-compliance. Companies wishing to do business in the USA have to be aware of the following legislation at least: Americans with Disabilities Act of 1990, section 225 of the Telecommunications Act of 1996, and the new section 508 of the Rehabilitation Act of 1973 (on Federal IT procurement) that came into effect 21 June 2001.

In the UK, much legislation is governed by EU directives. At the highest level, the Treaty of Amsterdam contains an important clause (article 13) on anti-discrimination, including age discrimination. This will see the UK introduce an anti-age discrimination law in the UK by 2006, but covering employment only.

At the Lisbon Summit meeting in 2000, the member states of the EU agreed an eEurope strategy 'for the EU to become the most dynamic knowledge-based economy in the world by 2010'. One of the targets was that all EU member states agreed to make their public information services readily accessible by 2002 and they would be monitored against this commitment. As a consequence, member states now require that their governmental (national and local) websites conform to the standards of the Web Accessibility Initiative (WAI). Another target was the setting up of a European network of centres that would promote Design for All and develop a European syllabus in Design for All (see www.eaccessibility.org/national_contact_centres.html).

The UK Disability Discrimination Act 1995 is having a major impact on service delivery and access to shops and public buildings over a ten-year period as the successive aspects of the Act are applied. The final phase of implementation in October 2004 will give disabled members of the public equal rights of access to goods, facilities and services, which means that service providers will have a duty to make reasonable adjustments to the physical features of their premises in order to comply. Yet the DDA applies only to the provision of services, and not directly to products except inasmuch as they may be the vehicles for service delivery. Currently, there is no statutory obligation on companies selling products in the UK to design accessible products, although the Disability Rights Commission plans to seek a commitment from the Government to extend disability rights legislation. There is some anecdotal evidence from the USA, however, that one of the effects in the short term of product legislation is that it becomes the (minimum) standard to which everyone works, with a stultifying effect on product innovation and consumer choice. As an example of this, it is not unknown for mobile phone companies to offer different variants of a phone in different countries, merely meeting the legislative accessibility requirements in those countries that demand it.

Standards

The range of standards and standards-making activities is immense and bears on companies' operating practices in a number of ways. Standards can apply nationally (eg BSI – British Standards Institution), regionally (eg ETSI – European Telecommunication Standards Institute, CENELEC – Committee for Electrotechnical Standardisation) or on a global basis (eg ISO – International Standards Organisation). They can be applied to products, processes and performance (absolute or in conjunction with a human user). They can be legally binding (ie underpinned by legislation), advisory or examples of good practice. They may be used at all stages of business or commercial processes. Finally, they may come about as a result of action by standards bodies, consumer pressure, consensus among interested parties or de facto through the market strength of a particular company. Normally, a standard drawn up and ratified by an established standards body carries more commercial clout than one that is not.

From an inclusive design perspective, there are relatively few instances to date of relevant standards. Prime examples are the UK Building Regulations Part M governing new housing (revision under review) and the WAI guidelines drawn up by the Web Accessibility

Initiative on how to design accessible websites. The international standards bodies ISO and IEC (International Electrotechnical Commission) have published a set of guidelines on how standards making should take account of the needs of older and disabled people. EU standards bodies CEN/CENELEC and ETSI were mandated under an eEurope accessibility initiative to investigate the possibilities for standards for design for all. This guide is now published as an ISO/IEC document. Whilst this is a useful step towards mainstreaming the issue of designing for disabled and older consumers, it remains to be seen how well these guidelines are adhered to without legal backup at national, European or global levels. The standards makers acknowledge the vast amount of work that has to be done before they can produce design for all product standards in areas where the technology is changing rapidly.

A different approach is currently being taken in the UK where a new BSI standard in the 7000 series on design management is being prepared that will look at inclusive design at all stages of the business life cycle. This is likely to be a more productive way forward, as a process standard can be applied to different markets and products in a technology-independent manner. This standard was issued for public comment in the summer of 2004, with publication of the full standard anticipated in June 2005.

Customer feedback

Customer feedback comes in many forms. It may be either positive or negative; it's hardly ever neutral! There is no doubt that the extreme form of negative feedback from dissatisfied customers and publicity in the media usually has a very powerful effect on the buying habits of customers and on the subsequent sales of the afflicted product. Negative feedback received directly by a company via its helplines or from guarantee claims is also a valuable source of information, but only organisations that have a strong customer-focused approach are able to use this feedback to best effect. This implies that an organisation that does not have strong user-centred processes already in place is unlikely to be susceptible to adopting a more inclusive design approach to its business.

The best form of customer feedback is to obtain it at an early stage of the design process where it can most easily have a direct impact on the product. Reworking a design to make a product more usable costs considerably more when the product is in the market, compared with doing it early in the design process. Software engineering studies show that the average user interface (the part of the product with which the user interacts directly) has 40 flaws. Correcting the easiest 20 yields an average task performance improvement of 50 per cent. The biggest gains occur when usability is factored in from the beginning, yielding as much as seven-fold improvements in efficiency such as time to complete a task. Attending to the users in the design process may add around 2 per cent to development costs, which should be recovered easily from additional sales. However, the published literature to date contains little quantifiable benefit or case studies on the benefit of using older or disabled people in an inclusive design process.

Competitive advantage

Seeking competitive advantage is a major business driver and the subject of many management books and courses. Inclusive design can provide competitive advantage in products by incorporating features that make products more usable and attractive to a larger number of people and hence increasing market share. This assumes that making the design suitable for less-able-bodied people does not detract from the attractiveness of the product to its prime market. Inclusive design may be a particularly attractive option for a non-dominant supplier in a market.

However, the failure of many products to meet the needs of older people is seldom due to deliberate action on the part of the designer or product manager. It is more likely to arise from unconscious prejudice, ignorance or a lack of awareness of the potential marketplace or customers. There is also the rush to get a new model to market in fast-moving product sectors. Many designers and product marketing managers are relatively young, without the direct experience of the ageing process and its consequences. When considering which product features to include, design and marketing decisions need to be based on hard evidence of the numbers of people who may be included or excluded by the decision to include a particular product feature and hence the likely impact on market share. Currently, there are few tools that enable decision-makers to assess the market impact of (inaccessible) features within their products caused by a failure in design to address the effects of impairments on human performance. However, tools are now beginning to appear that are a valuable step in bridging the divide between the quantitative world of business and the qualitative one of (inclusive) design.

In cases where the decision to produce an inclusively designed product is obvious, or the cost of doing so is small, product management and design decisions may not need to be backed up by quantitative data. Where safety is involved, it is vital to understand the users and the potential use of the product so that the wrong users are not included. For example, in the case of potentially hazardous substances such as pharmaceuticals and household cleaning fluids, making a product unusable by a child may also make it unusable by an older person. Here it is the packaging of the product rather than the actual product itself that is of importance. This example highlights the need for a more explicit approach to exclusion by design by designers and product managers – too often this happens by default, not by design.

Brand

Brands and the images they produce in the minds of customers (both actual and potential) are powerful tools in the strategic marketing of products and services. The impact of the total product offering on the customer is all-important; there is no point in designing an easy-to-use domestic appliance if it is unsafe, unreliable or plain ugly! The brand image is affected by many things: by the direct experience of using a product, by the product collateral (manuals, leaflets, etc), by the backup service and by advertising. It is notable that in a number of cases of successful inclusive design – this usually means commercial success that a company will talk about – there is no mention in the product advertising and literature of design for older or disabled people. This is perhaps not surprising. From the customers' perspective, they are treated no differently from anyone else – they are being mainstreamed. However, from the suppliers' perspective, it is unlikely that such altruism is the predominant factor. It is much more likely to be the consequence of a preconceived anxiety that association with older consumers will stigmatise the product in the eyes of the young.

However, such preconceptions can change. For instance, the marketing of cars used to emphasise performance and lifestyle aspects. Safety features were not mentioned because of the presumption that this would prompt anxiety about risk that would detract from the overall message. All this changed, however, once Volvo had shown that safety features could be sold to consumers. Now airbags, for example, are prominently featured in car advertisements, even though they are not required to meet regulatory requirements.

We are likely to see the promotion of inclusive design first in markets that are affected by legislation. The Finnish lift manufacturer Kone is a case in point. On its website (www.kone.com), it claims early conformance to the European standard on lift accessibility, especially for people with disabilities. In the UK, the company explains how it can help its customers meet the requirements of the Disability Discrimination Act. Kone goes further on its corporate website, however (search on 'accessibility'). It describes the importance of its Design for All approach to lift design, manufacture and installation. It has also identified a market opportunity arising from the ageing population – a range of lifts that can be easily retrofitted to existing buildings where there are no lifts. Kone believes that installing lifts in buildings without them may be the single most effective way to reduce the number of people being consigned to expensive health-care facilities and thereby extend the period of independent living for senior citizens and people with limited mobility.

It used to be the case that people would buy consumer durable products on retirement 'to see them through'. With earlier retirement and a longer post-retirement period, larger numbers of older people are likely to have to replace their consumer durables, having experienced some of the problems of growing old. Is there a market opportunity to create an inclusive brand to which older consumers would return when they needed replacement consumer durables?

Inclusive design – case study

The Ford Focus is an interesting example of a study of inclusive design. In the 1990s, Ford's management became aware of the ageing population, and the marketing data showed that a significant number of its cars were purchased by older people. Ford embarked on a research programme to find out what it needed to do to make its cars easier to drive and hence more attractive to the older market segment. One of the interesting things the company did was to provide its designers with a 'Third Age suit'.

This body suit, with gloves and goggles, restricted movements of joints and limbs, limited dexterity and simulated the effects of declining eyesight through yellowing glasses. This had the effect of making the designers more aware of the difficulties older people experienced getting into, driving and using their cars. The result of this research was a set of ergonomic principles that are now applied to the design of the interiors of all Ford cars. The Ford Focus was the first car to employ these principles. Once launched, the Focus became an instant success, jumping straight to the top of the best-selling car list in the UK, and subsequently becoming the world's best-selling car.

Despite its application of inclusive design principles, Ford's marketing material gives very little attention to this aspect of its design, although a number of articles have appeared in newspapers and trade journals. The car sells well to the under-35-year-old market, so its design to accommodate the needs of older drivers has not damaged its appeal to motorists of all ages. There is an interesting truism in the motor trade: 'You can sell a young man's car to an old man, but you can't sell old man's car to a young man.' Someone has also commented: 'You can't even sell an old man's car to an old man!' Given the prevailing attitudes in society and the importance of image to the sale and promotion of cars, it is not surprising that Ford chose not to emphasise the inclusive design aspect of its car, despite its deliberate attempts to design one that would appeal to all age groups. Without access to Ford's market research figures, it is hard to judge the impact of the inclusive design approach on the car's marketing success. Indeed, it may be the case that inclusive design principles can succeed only by stealth, becoming an accepted part of good design practice.

Mass customisation ● ● ● ● ● ● ● ● ● ● ● ●

An alternative approach to providing mainstream products that can be used by a large proportion of the population, without modification or adaptation, is to customise products to meet an individual customer's requirements at the manufacturing stage. This approach is called *mass customisation* and enables individually customised products to be produced at close to mass production prices. The technique is already being applied to cars, computers, shoes, housing and clothing, and can be expected to permeate many markets in years to come.

Mass customisation bridges the previously incompatible concepts of mass production and customisation. Mass production provided low cost at the expense of uniformity. 'Any colour as long as it's black' was Henry Ford's slogan when he first introduced mass production techniques to the motor industry. This thinking results in product exclusion if the needs of all potential customers are not taken into account in the design process. On the other hand, customised products that do meet individual needs often required skilled craftsmanship, putting such products out of the financial reach of all but the richest. Mass customisation enables companies to satisfy 'markets of one' for everyone – that is, at prices everyone can afford. Typically, mass production involves building products for stock, whereas mass customisation is building products to order and requires a different business model for its successful operation.

The key component is involving the customer early in the design process. Take, for example, Dell Computers. Potentially, every Dell computer is made to order and the computers are sold direct to customers with no retailer in the supply chain. The Internet has provided an easy way for customers to specify their requirements and place their orders direct with the manufacturer; previously it could be done only by phone.

A number of car manufacturers (Ford, Saab, BMW, VW, Renault) enable customers to 'design', 'build' or 'configure' their own cars via the Internet and view the results on their computer screens. This is possibly more a matter of mass personalisation, and the manufacturers do not yet accept orders direct; the potential customer still has to liaise with a dealer in order to obtain his or her car.

Mass customisation is a response to greater competition in global markets and is seen as a way of providing product differentiation and competitive advantage. It is also a response to our more diversified lifestyles and the continuing rising expectations of greater consumer choice. Given the heterogeneous nature of the older population, as we have seen in earlier chapters, mass customisation may well be a powerful technique in developing product markets for older people.

As an example of how things are developing, Bodymetrics in the UK has already conducted a trial in a London West End clothing store of new scanning technology that enables a shopper's body to be scanned within the store. The resultant three-dimensional body image is processed to derive body measurements that can be used either to determine which size of off-the-peg garments will fit the shopper best or to specify the measurements for a made-to-measure garment (digital tailoring). The customer can then use a virtual mannequin (three-dimensional computer image) to see what the chosen (virtual) clothes might look like before trying real clothes. The body measurements can then be stored on a database to be retrieved on future shopping trips or from home, enabling a customer to 'try on' clothes using software running on their home PC. Not only is the approach likely to revolutionise clothes shopping, as the company claims, it will also make it much easier for people with disabilities or with restricted mobility to purchase clothes that fit, at prices close to mass market clothing. It also enables these people to shop in exactly the same way as other people; there is no reason for them to be treated any differently.

Mass customisation should not be thought of as an alternative to inclusive design – it is likely to be an additional means by which more inclusively designed products will be delivered to the market if suppliers seize the opportunity. The inclusive design approach is still required to ensure that customisation can meet the needs of as wide a range of customers as is economically viable. This approach is being taken by Fiat in its Autonomy Programme. This programme, launched in 1995, covers the design of the whole range of Fiat vehicles, including, for example, low-loading buses. Specialist fittings and devices have been developed that accommodate the needs of a wide range of disabled car-users, not just drivers; for example, swivelling car seats to make getting in and out of a car easier. An important part of the programme is a European-wide network of mobility centres where potential customers can try out the various forms of fitting required. The Autonomy Programme is responsible for the sale of over 20,000 cars per year, and so represents a valuable business opportunity to the Fiat Group. The programme is gradually moving its business model from one of special adaptations to one of low-cost cars with a high degree of adaptability that the company hopes will cover the whole population – a truly inclusive approach that is an integral part of Fiat's business strategy.

Implications ● ● ● ● ● ● ● ● ● ● ● ● ● ●

The needs of many older people are not very different from those of the population as a whole. They certainly don't want to be thought of as different. Creating inclusively designed products may not mean a large extension in market size but, in these days of tight margins, the extra percentage point of market share is worth having, especially if you are not the market leader. The manufacturing techniques of mass customisation may make smaller market sizes worth pursuing.

Times are changing because of legislation and standards. Inclusivity is 'in' and it may be possible to build a strong competitive edge out of inclusively designed products, even though they may have to be marketed carefully for a while to avoid alienating younger consumers. Creating a mainstream product brand around ease of use makes more sense in a marketplace where there will be larger numbers of older and more experienced customers. With increased longevity, larger numbers of older people will be in the market for replacement mainstream consumer goods.

Further reading

Bias, G.R. and Mayhew, D.J. (1994) *Cost-justifying Usability*. New York: Academic Press

British Standards Institution. (2005) *Design Management Systems: guide to managing inclusive design*, BS7000-6. London: BSI (For progress on this Standard, search for BSI Project 2002/02907 on webserv.bsi-global.com/projectline/

Connell, B.R., Jones, M., Mace, R., et al. (1997) *The Principles of Universal Design* (www.design.ncsu.edu/cud/univ_design/ principles/udprinciples.htm)

Coughlin, J. (2002) *MIT's AgeLab Helps Industry Redefine the Business of Old Age* (web.mit.edu/agelab/news_events/pdfs/ mitreport_oct2002.pdf)

Chisholm, W., Vanderheiden, G. and Jacobs, I. (1999) *Web Content Accessibility Guidelines 1.0* (www.w3.org/TR/1999/WAI-WEBCONTENT-19990505/)

Disability Rights Commission. (2004) *Strategic Plan 2004–2007* (www.drc-gb.org/whatwedo/oppdetails.asp?id=36)

eAccessibility (www.eaccessibility.org/national_contact_centres.html)

Ford, R. (2000) 'Auto designs for the ages', *Boston Globe* newspaper, USA, May 3, A01 (architecture.mit.edu/house_n/web/ resources/articles/transgenerational/cars.htm)

Gilmore, J.H. and Pine, B.J. (eds). (2000) *Markets of One: creating customer-unique value through mass customization*. Cambridge MA: Harvard Business School Press

International Standards Organization (2002) *Guidelines for standards developers to address the needs of older persons and persons with disabilities*, ISO/IEC GUIDE 71 (2001-2) Ed. 1.0 (www.domino.iec.ch/webstore/webstore.nst/artnum/028381)

Keates, S. and Clarkson, J.P. (2003) *Countering Design Exclusion: an introduction to inclusive design*. London: Springer-Verlag

Kone (www.kone.com)

Landauer, T.K. (1996) *The Trouble with Computers: usefulness, usability and productivity*. Cambridge MA: MIT Press

SENIORWATCH. (2002) *Final Report* (www.empirica.biz/swa/)

Underwood, M.J. and Metz, D.H. (2003) *Seven Business Drivers of Inclusive Design*. Proceedings of INCLUDE 2003 'Inclusive Design for Society and Business', Helen Hamlyn Research Centre, Royal College of Art, CD-ROM ISBN 1 874175 94 2 11, obtainable from Helen Hamlyn Research Centre

7 Addressing the special needs of ageing

In this chapter we look at the market for satisfying the needs arising from the personal consequences of the ageing process. This is a very diverse market, ranging from traditional assistive technologies, through smart homes, to mainstream systems that enable older people to continue as active citizens. In future, these markets are likely to be driven both by technological developments and by increased pressure on social services arising from the needs of larger numbers of older people. Older people with more money will be keen to spend it on making their lives more comfortable. It is unlikely that the state can ever be relied on to provide everything that is needed in our old age.

The Royal Commission on Long Term Care defined assistive technology as 'an umbrella term for any device or system that allows an individual to perform a task they would otherwise be unable to do, or increases the ease and safety with which the task can be performed'. This broad definition covers a very wide range of products addressing the diverse needs of individuals according to their personal circumstances (see Table 7.1).

The Royal Commission described the aims of assistive technology as fourfold – to help people:

- maintain autonomy and dignity;
- pursue self-fulfillment;
- lead an independent life;
- remain a valued member of society.

Common conditions affecting people over 65	Incidence in the population	Assistive technologies that can help alleviate the condition and help to maintain independence
Arthritis	50%	Equipment for daily living
Hypertension and heart disease	30%	Wheelchairs; telehealth for remote monitoring of vital signs such as heart rate and variability and body weight
Diabetes	11%	Orthopaedic footwear; telehealth for remote monitoring of blood glucose, hypoglycaemia alarms and medication reminders
Hearing problems	32%	Hearing aids, induction loops, textphones
Cataracts and other forms of visual degeneration	26%	Visual aids, better lighting, reading magnification cameras and displays, colour sensors, text-to-sound converters
Mobility problems	35%	Wheelchairs, walking frames, stair-lifts, fall detectors, bed monitors, personal environmental controls
Dementia	5%	Telecare systems to monitor safety and movement

(From Audit Commission (2004) *Assistive Technology, Independence and Well-being 4*, London, Audit Commission)

Table 7.1 Common ailments/conditions that can be helped by the use of assistive technology

Taking a more commercially orientated perspective, we have chosen three broad sub-categories based upon the primary needs of the individual:

■ personal devices addressing one or more functional impairments, such as hearing loss or impaired mobility;

■ independent living, enabling older people to live longer in their own homes;

■ systems that enable older people to live worthwhile lives as members of society.

Addressing functional impairments ● ● ● ● ● ● ●

The origins of this form of assistive technology are not new. Walking sticks and glasses are obvious examples, having existed in one form or another for centuries. Products addressing functional impairments are usually highly personal in nature, and, although they exist largely as self-contained devices, the more high-tech variants do need to work with other kinds of equipment. For example, people with hearing aids still like to use a telephone. Whilst many telephones have been designed for use with hearing aids, digital mobile phones frequently interfere with the older style of analogue hearing aid, much to the despair of their users. In other words, a mainstream approach has to be taken to the design of assistive technology devices, taking into account the wider needs of the user and the context within which these devices will be used.

The old image of assistive technology of all kinds is one of functionally orientated products that frequently have a stigma associated with them because of poor design. Traditionally, many small specialist companies operating in small markets have made many of these products – a clear case of market fragmentation. The low level of investment available has frequently led to products that do not look attractive, cost more than they should, with poor service and support. Poor reliability and functionality have been found to be major factors influencing people against using assistive technology devices even after they have been provided with them.

Good design is also important for older people, as they do not like to be thought of as disabled or reminded of their failing bodies or minds. The way in which many of these products have traditionally been purchased has been a major factor in their design; products have been purchased by one group of people (eg social services departments) for another group of people – the users. These two groups of people often have conflicting needs. In the case of mass purchase by a large authority, the end-user invariably has little say in the selection process. The consequence is products designed primarily to meet cost constraints rather than the end-users' requirements of acceptability, usability or effectiveness. A stark reminder of this was the woman who refused to accept an artificial leg because it could not be provided in a colour to match her dark skin without a very significant surcharge; only pink legs were available on the NHS. The situation is changing, as larger numbers of older people with purchasing power are becoming both the user and the purchaser, with consequent changes in the factors companies have to address. This represents a market opportunity for better, less stigmatising, assistive technology products.

The new image and style of assistive technology products is rather different, however, from both a technological and a purchasing perspective. Some markets for assistive technology products are very significant and high tech. Take, for example, glasses. The optical retailing market in the UK is worth about £2 billion per annum. The production of individually prescribed lenses, especially Varifocal lenses, is now a high-tech volume business. Whether the opticians and lens manufacturers would regard themselves as being in the assistive technology business is another matter, however! In Italy, some 20 per cent of spectacles sold are fitted with plain glass, an assistive technology device that has become a fashion accessory. This is not unlike Victorian times, when walking sticks were a fashion accessory – might they come back into vogue?

Another good example embracing advanced technology is hearing aids. More than half the population over 60 years of age has some kind of hearing impairment. The latest hearing aids involve sophisticated digital signal processing technology implemented in state-of-the-art microelectronics combined with long-life batteries and low weight. Together these developments mean that hearing aids can be designed to fit into the ear (where they are not visible, thereby reducing the stigma associated with being seen to wear one), can be tailored to an individual's hearing loss and can be adjusted by the wearer to suit listening in different acoustic environments. Until recently, digital hearing aids were very expensive and not available on the NHS. As from October 2003, digital hearing aids have been available under the NHS at a cost to the NHS of £65 for an average powered aid. The advances in microelectronics and other manufacturing techniques mean that it is possible to produce disposable hearing aids, that you throw away after about 40 days when the battery fails – a far cry from the hearing trumpet of the Middle Ages! One claimed advantage is that a person can try out a hearing aid at relatively low cost to see how well it meets their needs.

With advances in information and communication technologies (ICTs), assistive technology products are no longer confined to dealing with mainly physical and sensory impairments. Synthetic speech devices built into hand-held computers or personal digital assistants are giving people who have lost the ability to speak (eg because of a stroke) the opportunity to communicate more easily with other people. Hand-held computers can be programmed to act as reminder devices for people with memory loss. As we learn more about the operation of the human mind, we are likely to see more devices capable of helping people with differing aspects of dementia. It is important that these devices be readily customisable to individual need, quite possibly on an on-going basis. Manufacturers will need to either ensure that the devices can be tailored without recourse to highly trained staff or provide the necessary support service for customisation and updating as part of their product offering.

Another major problem in the supply of this category of assistive technology devices is the range of impairments a product has to accommodate. Targeting a product too narrowly at a particular aspect results in a small market. At the other extreme, by the very nature of functional impairments, one design would certainly not fit all. A careful balance has to be struck. The problem has been solved for most of the common hearing and vision problems of old age, whereby devices can be manufactured to meet individual needs. Advanced manufacturing techniques now being developed enable individual products to be made either from a mould (eg to make a replacement part) or from a digital specification. Siemens, the world's largest manufacturer of hearing aids, is in the process of switching the manufacture of nylon hearing-aid shells to such a process. Pilot production has confirmed that computer-controlled laser machines can fabricate shells from nylon dust, resulting in better fit, performance and quality at lower cost. Further developments in 'instant manufacturing' will make small production runs more economic, thereby making it easier to produce specialised, highly customised, assistive devices.

Continuing advances in medical technologies and microelectronics in the future are likely to lead to further improvements in the range of conditions that can be helped by assistive technology. In the 1980s the first cochlear implants were available that converted amplified electronic signals from a microphone directly into nerve impulses, bypassing diseased or failed parts of the hearing mechanism. Hearing is only the first sensory process to benefit from neurostimulation implants, and a wide range of implants is being researched worldwide to replace the effects of damaged nerves on muscular control for activities such as walking, manual control, etc. Development of these smaller, less invasive, bodily sensors with those in the IT world, such as wearable computers or smart clothing, is likely to create new opportunities for assistive technology devices in the future.

The need for independence and control at home

The majority of older people express the wish to continue living in their own home for as long as possible. It is usually some major life event, such as the loss of a life-long partner, serious illness or disability, that forces people to reconsider that decision. Currently, some 9–10 per cent of people of pensionable age live in special settings (sheltered housing, care homes, etc), whilst around 25 per cent of people over the age of 85 live in special settings. Evidence to the Royal Commission on Long Term Care showed that the cost of caring for older people in their own homes (with domiciliary care) was usually the least expensive option for the state.

As the population ages, pressure on already hard-pressed social services departments to fund long-term care is going to increase, both because of increased demand (larger numbers of older people) and decreased supply (smaller numbers of younger people to provide the care at the comparatively low salaries offered). This in turn will increase the pressure for older people staying in their own home for as long as they can. As always, the key question is how long this remains a viable option, for as people become frailer they require increasing assistance from formal or informal carers. At the very minimum they have to be able carry out the activities of daily living (ADLs), which include such tasks as dressing, bathing, eating, toileting, transfer (eg from bed to chair) and walking. A huge variety of aids are already available to help people carry out these and associated activities, many relatively simple, inexpensive and effective in use. Examples include kitchen utensils, bath aids, walking aids, adapted toilets and stair-lifts. A recent Audit Commission report makes the financial case for the highly cost-effective nature of many of these aids. For example, fitting a bath that someone can use on their own is very cost-effective compared with providing a personal service to bathe them. However, there is also the question of who pays for the modifications to the home – the individual, the relatives or the local authority – as the different stakeholders have different perceptions of costs, benefits and responsibility.

Older people have additional requirements that need to be satisfied if they are to continue living independently and exercise control over their own living environment. Control is probably the primary motivating issue here, rather than one of independence. Independence implies lack of dependence on other people. Control can be exercised through the purchase of services from other people. The list of additional needs includes:

- daily management of the house (eg controlling who enters);

- household cleaning and clothes washing;

- shopping – purchase of food and other essential items;

- management of money;

- house maintenance, including gardening;

- ability to summon help and/or acquire other services.

A wide range of easier-living products is available to enable people to carry out the tasks themselves, ranging from simple tools such as tap turners, grab rails, jar openers, good-grip kitchen utensils and tools with long handles through to advanced technological aids at the other extreme. Again, the importance of attractive products cannot be over-emphasised, as older people are resistant to the installation of aids and adaptations that draw attention to their reduced competence and self-sufficiency. Many manufacturers have reacted to the challenge but we feel that there is an untapped growth market for stylish designs and products that make everyday-living tasks easier.

Internet shopping and banking have made it possible for many people, whether housebound or not, to carry out information-based transactions from the comfort of their own homes at a time and in a manner they find convenient. Neither Internet shopping nor banking could have been cost-justified for older people alone but there is no doubt that they have made a significant difference to the lives of many people who are no longer as active as they used to be. Again, the importance of adherence to good inclusive design principles in these applications cannot be over-emphasised.

An important aspect of life for an older person living alone is the ability to summon help when needed. Social alarms have been developed, mainly for emergency purposes, which enable people to use a 24-hour service to call the sheltered housing warden, the local social services or even the emergency services. There are now over 1.5 million people in the UK served by such systems. However, these work only if the person is physically able to summon the services via a call-centre – they may have had a fall in a position where they cannot reach their emergency call system, hence the use of emergency pendants worn round the neck or devices worn on the wrist.

Social alarm systems are now being fitted with fall detectors. An electronic sensor worn by the user detects the sudden change from the vertical to horizontal position of the wearer and, via a radio link to the telephone, dials the call centre. Receiving rapid medical attention is a major factor in effecting the subsequent mobility of a person after treatment. Some 90 per cent of older people who have a major fall can subsequently live independently if they receive help in the first hour after the fall. Without effective treatment, there is the real danger that a person who has had a fall may enter the spiral of decreasing mobility and increasing risk of falling, with associated loss of quality of life and increased demands on the caring services. The current cost of hip fractures in the UK is reckoned to be £725 million per year, 50 per cent of which is spent in social care. One in three people over the age of 65 suffers a fall each year, and two-thirds of them suffer another fall in the next six months.

The range of personal health-monitoring equipment whose data can be transmitted to hospitals is also growing. Vital-signs monitors (measuring temperature, blood pressure, pulse rate, breathing rate and oxygen level) connected to patients at home transmit data to the hospital, enabling people to be released safely from hospital at an earlier point in their treatment. Early implementation of these systems is underway in a number of parts of the UK.

To date, many of the developments in home-based systems have taken place in an ad hoc manner, with separate unconnected systems addressing different needs. Many of these technological possibilities are now being brought together under the concept of the Smart Home, the definition of which is 'A dwelling incorporating a communications network that connects the key electrical appliances and services, and allows them to be remotely controlled, monitored or accessed.' Remotely means from inside or outside the building. The main components of a smart home are: a network for communication; a gateway (basically a computer) to manage the system; and automation products inside and outside the home.

The smart home concept is now becoming as applicable to existing dwellings as to new-build, because the growth of wireless technology means it is no longer necessary to hardwire a house to install a communications network. Six main application areas are envisaged:

- environmental control;
- security and access;
- home entertainment;

- domestic appliances;

- information and communication;

- health (telecare and home assistance).

In the context of independent living for older people, it is the telecare and home assistance applications that are of the most relevance. Telecare has three main objectives: enabling a person to live independently, summon help when required and anticipate accidents before they happen (eg detect that a gas ring has not been turned off). The following is a list of some of the envisaged application areas:

- occupant monitoring (eg falls, getting up on time);

- medication reminders;

- health monitoring (eg blood pressure, diabetes);

- entry phone system, perhaps linked to television;

- daily routine reminders.

As an example of the kind of benefit to be obtained from one of these components, a US trial of a computerised medication-reminder system showed that it increased patients' compliance with medication from 34 per cent to 94 per cent, with an associated reduced admission rate to hospitals for those with congestive heart failure of 41 per cent. This is a clear benefit to both the individual and those providing health care.

Trials of smart homes have been undertaken for a number of years, driven mainly by a futuristic view of what it might be possible to deliver, as opposed to what would make a difference to the residents and therefore they would be willing to pay for. One of the major problems is a lack of documented understanding of what happens in the domestic environment, such that it is possible to design technological solutions that meet real needs. The world of work has been studied extensively, but not the domestic environment in a way that would be helpful to product designers. What research there is points to the wide range of living styles, making it difficult to design products that will fit with the existing patterns of home behaviour. It is too much to expect people, especially older people, to adapt their living styles to the technology – it has to be the other way around.

The growth in the market for smart home technology and systems is likely to be incremental, both because of cost factors and so that people can grow their home systems as they renovate parts of the home or as their requirements change. The investment in the technology is substantial, including the all-important standards by which everything would communicate over the home network, and will involve the co-operation of companies from a number of markets with interests in the home. The demands of the larger numbers of older people may well be insufficient to warrant the investment required. However, the provision of an infrastructure that would enable specific devices to be attached in a flexible manner would lower the cost of entry to the market for devices of particular interest to older people. For example, a system providing advanced security features to a home provides all the basic infrastructure to enable personal health monitoring.

The Department of Trade and Industry sponsored a project at the Millennium Homes in Greenwich to investigate how smart home technology could help older people with reduced abilities to stay in their own homes. Ten homes were packed with sensors to monitor all kinds of activity within the home, including detectors of unlit gas and over-running baths, commonplace occurrences with older people with dementia. The first residents were reported to be enthusiastic but there remain a number of long-term social issues to be evaluated. As with monitoring any kind of human activity, there are major technological, personal and ethical issues to be overcome.

From a technical perspective, it is hard to define what is 'normal' activity within a home so that abnormal activity can be reported. In the case of the Millennium Homes, the system would negotiate with the resident first before sending an external alarm message. If there were no response, for example to a synthesised speech message or the bath was not turned off, the appropriate alarm would be raised. However, assimilating normal patterns of behaviour so that abnormal ones can be detected reliably remains a difficult technical problem. Miniature biomedical sensors are also becoming available that will enable more health conditions to be monitored remotely, thereby enabling medical problems to be anticipated and treated early without the individual having to make the physical journey to the local health clinic.

An important issue is the acceptability of this kind of technology to the occupier. Today's older people have shown a willingness to use computers where they see a clear benefit, for instance to keep in touch with grandchildren or to pursue hobbies. Internet-based home shopping services have proved to be of great value for older people, especially those in rural communities. But older people are reported to be less enthusiastic about wider applications of technology that they do not trust. Future generations of older people seem perhaps less likely to have such misgivings. Even so, personal monitoring of the kind discussed here represents new territory.

A number of recent studies indicate how a range of individual economic, health and social gains might be made using advanced technology, whilst noting that considerably more investigation is needed to understand the real needs of users, as well as the ethical and legal considerations. However, there is no compelling evidence so far about the cost-effectiveness of this technology. If and when fully implemented, the more futuristic systems are likely to have a profound effect on how health and social services are delivered, involving significant job redesign in the process. Taken together, these factors mean that progress is likely to be slow rather than dramatic. Moreover, assistive technology devices in smart homes should be seen only as being complementary to other forms of care. Some technological pundits see robots as providing the answer to the caring problems in an ageing society – robots don't need food or sleep and are likely to be more obedient and tolerant servants than the most long-suffering relative or carer. Whether robots will be acceptable to future older people remains to be seen. Many people, not just older ones, would probably be quite happy to delegate menial household and garden tasks to robots.

However, in our view, robots able to carry out the personal caring needs of older people, such as washing and dressing, are a distant vision and likely to remain so.

Addressing social needs ● ● ● ● ● ● ● ● ● ●

It is important for the health and well-being of all people to maintain social engagement. This becomes especially difficult for older people in the face of declining physical capabilities. Maintaining social contact is recognised to be an important component of active ageing. Frequently, the major barriers to older people engaging in social activities occur in getting around outside their homes or accessing relevant information or communication channels. The way in which future products and services might be developed to address these needs is discussed in this section.

Social needs imply contact with other people. Historically, this has required physical transport over short, medium or longer distances, a topic considered in Chapter 8. Where physical mobility is difficult, one solution is to bring the resources to the people, for example in the form of mobile shops and libraries, and meals-on-wheels services. Shopping at a distance is popular with older consumers, traditionally using catalogues and nowadays increasingly via the Internet. Nevertheless, the desire to visit real shops is arguably part of the human condition, and indeed shopping trips, together with personal business, account for more than half of all journeys made by women in their late 60s and beyond, and for men from their early 70s. Once in the shopping centre, there is the problem of movement around the shops and facilities. As a result of recent changes in legislation and the development of better battery technology, more older people may now be seen whizzing around the community on their own motorised wheelchairs or scooters, or within shopping centres (using hired or borrowed machines). The market for battery-driven wheelchairs and scooters has grown from nothing 30 years ago to the point today where they are commonplace, with around 100,000 electric wheelchairs on the pavements and a similar number of scooters.

The second aspect that helps an older person with restricted mobility to travel is planning the journey, either in advance or during the journey itself. Visually impaired people have particular problems of knowing where they are, sufficient to deter many of them from venturing out alone. Although the Disability Discrimination Act requires transport providers to make their services accessible, planning a journey if you have one or more impairments is not as easy as it is for able-bodied people. For instance, it is essential to know which stations have working lifts or ramps. For a journey to be completed, every stage in the journey has to be manageable. A variety of research trials have taken place; for example, in North Tyneside information was disseminated via teletext about the provision of accessible features at railway stations, and to enable people to find when the next accessible bus would arrive at their nearest bus-stop.

There is considerable interest in the development of information and communication technologies to encourage the use of public transport. For instance, the Department for Transport is funding the development of 'Transport Direct', a sophisticated system that aims to provide the traveller with all the information they need before and during a journey anywhere in the UK, thus helping people to plan their journeys, to compare routes and prices across different types of transport, and to buy the associated tickets. This is a formidable undertaking, and the extent to which it will be possible to accommodate the needs of travellers with disabilities remains to be seen. Where such needs cannot be accommodated, there will be opportunities for the development of assistive technologies that interact both with the traveller and with the travel information system, thus enabling the former to benefit from the latter to the same extent as non-disadvantaged travellers.

Visually impaired people have particular problems in finding their way around strange environments – ones that they have not used before. Navigation systems for visually impaired people are now becoming available commercially using Geographic Positioning Systems (GPS). These were originally developed for military purposes, giving soldiers their position on the Earth's surface with an accuracy better than a few metres. Applications of the technology have spread to commercial use for sailors, cars and, more recently, personal navigation devices for the visually impaired. Combined with information from a Geographic Information System (think of this as a digital map) and speech synthesis, products are now available that enable a visually impaired person to navigate their way through town centres, go shopping and meet friends without assistance. Like the car-driver or walker, they can set up their own waypoints to re-use the route again in the future.

Simpler systems are now being installed at major shopping centres to provide information to visually impaired people with information about where they are. Sensors in the building detect signals from transmitters carried by these people (usually on loan from ShopMobility). Depending upon the type of system in use, the user will either hear a recorded voice in an earpiece or a broadcast message from a loudspeaker indicating where they are ('You are now standing outside Marks & Spencer'). These systems also have value for the emergency services, which might have to work in a strange building in smoke-filled conditions, and adds to the business case for installing them.

In the information age, access to services is increasingly mediated by information and communication technologies (ICTs), with virtual travel augmenting real travel. It is no longer necessary to make the physical journey to shop, visit relatives, etc. Television, telephones and, more recently, Internet technology (including email) have made it possible to carry out business and banking, and to maintain contact with relatives at a distance on a scale hitherto impossible. Again, the needs of older people are not radically different from those of younger people, so it will be important to ensure that their needs are not overlooked in the development of new services. An inclusive approach is required. Particular examples are looked at in the next chapter under the ICT key sector heading.

The Baby Boomer Bistro created by Age Concern was the first chat site in the UK developed specifically for people over 50. It offers chatters the chance to meet and make friends around the world. It also allows politicians, decision-makers and experts in many different fields to hear the voices of older people via a variety of special virtual events.

There is an interesting development in worship on the Internet in the USA and parts of Europe with low population densities and scattered communities (eg Finland). Church services are videoed for transmission live over the Internet or for playback on demand at a time that is more convenient. Sermons, church and community notices are also available for download. Not only does this enable people to take part in services in the community that they might not otherwise be able to do but it also provides them with a greater degree of choice, and indeed the possibility to join services in other countries.

Benefits for everyone of designing for older people ● ● ●

As this chapter has shown, there is a two-way movement of technology between special needs and mainstream markets. Not surprisingly, most of the technology applied to the needs of disabled or older people was originally developed for mainstream markets. However, there are instances of where the technology has moved in the other direction, from the specialised need to mainstream. An early example: Alexander Graham Bell was working on an early form of electrical hearing aid when he saw the possibility of his invention being used more widely for point-to-point communication as the telephone. The cassette tape recorder was introduced to help visually impaired people who had difficulty threading the reels of open spool tape recorders. This technology was subsequently refined to make it suitable for hi-fi use, and then became a dominant medium for the recording and replay of music until it was overtaken by the higher quality compact disc. Part of the original motivation behind Teletext was the need to help hearing-impaired people access television information.

A recent example is the predictive text input system used for SMS (texting) on mobile phones. This technology relies on the characteristics of human language to enable you to enter text with one key depression per character, although the individual keys on a phone may represent three or four characters. (The alternative is multiple key depressions per character.) This technology was originally developed in the 1980s to help people whose manual control did not allow them to use standard computer keyboards. It is somewhat ironic that a technique that was devised for people with very limited manual dexterity and control is now being applied to products that have been made so small that many people find them difficult to use!

Implications ● ● ● ● ● ● ● ● ● ● ● ● ●

- New technology is widening the scope for creating new types of better assistive technology products.

- New manufacturing techniques are being developed that will enable better customisation and the ability to meet the needs of small markets.

- There are market opportunities in providing new services, not just products.

- New patterns of supply are likely as richer older people are looking to find and fund assistive products for themselves.

Further reading

Abascal, J. (2003) 'Threats and opportunities of rising technologies for smart houses, in: CEN/CENELEC/ETSI Conference Proceedings Accessibility for All (www.etsi.org/cce/proceedings/3_2.htm)

Appleton, N.J.W. (2002) *Planning for the Majority: the needs and aspirations of older people in general housing*. London: Joseph Rowntree Foundation (also downloadable from www.jrf.org.uk/knowledge/findings/housing/pdf/N32.pdf)

Audit Commission. (2004) *Assistive Technology, Independence and Well-being 4*. London: Audit Commission

Brownsell, S. and Bradley, D. (2003) *Assistive Technology and Telecare*. Bristol: Policy Press

Cowan, D. and Turner-Smith, A. (1999) *The Role of Assistive Technology in Alternative Models of Care for Older People*, Royal Commission on Long Term Care, Appendix 4. London: The Stationery Office (see www.archive.official-documents.co.uk/ document/cm41/4192/v2ap4.pdf)

Curry, R.G., Trejo Tinoco, M. and Wardle, D. (2002) *The Use of Information and Communication Technology to support Independent Living for Older and Disabled People*. London: Department of Health (see www.icesdoh.org/downloads/ICT-Older-People-July-2003.pdf)

Department of Trade and Industry. (2003) *The Application Home Initiative* (see www.theapplicationhome.com/)

Harper, R. (ed). (2003) *Inside the Smart Home*. London: Springer-Verlag

Millennium Homes. (2003) (see www.ost.gov.uk/link/linkcasestudies/ millenniumhomesapril03.pdf)

SmartHome (see www.changeagentteam.org.uk/_library/docs/ housing/smarthome.pdf)

Sutherland S. (chair). (1999) *With Respect to Old Age*, The Royal Commission on Long Term Care. London: The Stationery Office (see www.archive.official-documents.co.uk/document/cm41/ 4192/4192.htm)

8 Key sectors

This chapter examines a number of key market sectors that we believe are particularly significant as far as older consumers are concerned. Inevitably, there is some overlap between this chapter and the immediately preceding chapters on mainstream markets and special needs markets. In those two chapters, we looked at the markets in broad terms and where they might be heading in the future. In this chapter, we look at individual sectors, consider what has been achieved in terms of meeting the needs of older customers and speculate on potential market opportunities. We have included examples of where to get information about the needs and characteristics of older customers and users. We have tried to illustrate the sectors with case studies to give some insight into what has been achieved and why. It has to be pointed out, however, that currently there is very little published material on business-orientated case studies that address the older customer – another market opportunity in itself, perhaps!

It is worth noting at this point that the classic marketing approach breaks the purchasers of products into five categories:

- Innovators – the first 5–10 per cent who adopt the product
- Early adopters – the next 10–15 per cent
- Early majority – the next 30 per cent
- Late majority – the next 30 per cent
- Laggards – the remaining 20 per cent

Innovators and early adopters are usually considered to be crucial for launching new products. As purchasers, they are more likely to be concerned with getting the new product, showing other people they have the new product, etc, than they are with issues such as the usability of the product. Older people, on the other hand, tend to be more concerned with value and quality (fitness for purpose), so consequently do not usually figure among the early adopters of a product, unless there is considerable advantage to them. It follows that, generally, new products are not designed initially for older people; they are expected to follow in the early or late majority, when the technology is becoming more mature and the selling points no longer stress the novelty of technology, rather other aspects such as ease of use. The interesting question is whether demographic developments will change this in any way, as the relative numbers of younger people fall, thereby changing the characteristics of the early adopter market. Does this mean that new products will have to move faster up the usability curve on introduction to attract the larger numbers of older purchases earlier in the product life cycle than happens at present? As we discuss later, the evidence that this might be happening – for instance, as with the introduction of digital television – is not encouraging.

Leisure

For many people, reaching retirement is the time when they can concentrate on doing what they want to do, health permitting. For some, this is the chance to spend more time pursuing hobbies and pastimes developed over a lifetime; for others, it is the opportunity to develop new interests; yet others choose to engage in part-time work (paid or unpaid) to sustain their social contacts (or income). For many, there is the likelihood of being a grandparent that may result in more travel and different purchasing patterns; for instance, toys and clothes for the grandchildren. Many companies in the leisure sector have already started to develop their business to take advantage of the increased leisure time and wealth of today's retired people. As we have pointed out elsewhere, today's retired people pursue much more varied lifestyles than did their parents, largely because they have more disposable income and better health.

Many of the interests of older people are shared by younger members of the population, so new leisure markets specifically addressing older people seem most unlikely. Rather, it is a case of developing market niches targeted towards older people, mainly in terms of exploiting the time they have available or the activities they like to pursue. A common approach is to exploit off-peak times of the day, week or year when facilities are otherwise under-used and therefore not earning revenue. Ways of addressing this opportunity include pensioner discount cards (eg 10 per cent off on Tuesdays in certain DIY stores and garden centres) and membership schemes, such as the Beefeater Inns' Emerald Card scheme that allows discounts and alternative menus for people over 55 outside the weekend or evening periods. Travel discounts are available with a Senior Rail Card, the advertising for which is a good example of the marketing approach. It shows a child on holiday and asks, 'When was the last time you could do what you wanted?' and suggests that you can again with a Senior Rail Card.

Attracting older customers in this way makes good business sense by using spare capacity in off-peak periods, and making an attractive offer can bring in worthwhile returns for business. It is probably one of the few ways in which age-based advertising and promotion works with older people, by making it an advantage to be their age. This is an uncommon experience for older people in today's society.

Homes and gardens

Studies show that a significant number of people devote more time to some aspects of home improvement when they retire. The reasons are not hard to find. They will be spending more time in their homes than previously, so the outdated kitchens or bedrooms are more noticeable; they might not have had time to do it before or they feel the need to do it before they are no longer able to do so. For people moving when they retire, either to be nearer their family or to live in a more pleasant environment, this later life nest-building urge is likely to be even stronger. Those with enough money and insufficient skills or inclination will be looking for other people to do the work for them. As the number of older people increases, the demand for decorators, home improvement companies, jobbing builders and landscape gardeners is likely to grow, further exacerbating the current skills shortages in these areas.

Both garden centres and DIY stores have succeeded in attracting additional older customers on certain days of the week with senior discount cards. Many garden centres have found it profitable to run cafés and restaurants that are staffed on weekdays as well as weekends, having discovered that older people go to garden centres during the week, and not just in the summer months. In 2002, B&Q launched a series of light and easy-to-use power tools suitable for older people and women, as distinct from the more professional power tools they also sell. This complements the policy B&Q have pursued for a number of years in employing older people in their stores and warehouses. They have identified a variety of business benefits from this, including greater staff retention, less pilferage by staff and, significantly from a business perspective, a greater willingness by customers to consult members of staff their own age on some aspect of DIY. Surprisingly (to some) they found that older people were better learners of the use of in-store tills and procedures.

Gardening is reported to be the nation's favourite pastime and for older people is the most popular form of exercise after walking. Readership of gardening magazines is weighted towards the over-50s, although this is not the impression to be gained from reading the magazines. Gardening is an example of an inclusive market and activity – one that can be carried out or enjoyed by people of all ages on a scale consistent with their physical strength and inclination. For it is not just doing one's own garden that is popular, visiting other people's gardens and those of large houses (owned by the National Trust, for example) is also very popular. Indeed, this interest in gardens probably extends beyond those who are active gardeners. However, as we note elsewhere, the inability to maintain a garden is a very visible sign of an older person's increasing frailty and is often a cause of worry to older people when they are no longer able to cope.

Fitness

There is ample evidence that keeping fit and supple in old age is a good way to protect the body from a number of medical problems such as high blood pressure, heart disease and osteoporosis, as well as helping to prevent falls and broken bones. Increasing numbers of older people are now joining health clubs and gyms, with the result that the industry claims that pensioners are the fastest-growing group in society becoming members of gyms and sports clubs. Gyms have become the latest business sector to realise that there is money to be made from the grey market. Discount rates and gentler exercise and music have been part of the attraction. A number of gyms now run specific off-peak programmes tailored to the needs of older people.

For example, LA Fitness, one of the UK's largest gym chains, started to address older members in 2001 with a series of classes intended for older people, called Prime Time. It realised that it had to change both the marketing message and the style of activities offered in the gyms if it were to attract older members. For many years, the fitness clubs had placed the emphasis on youth, beauty, muscles and fitness, best summed up as being part of the 'Lycra scene'. This was not an attractive message to potential older members and actively discouraged many from joining. Exercise regimens and music are both toned down to suit older daytime members and there is greater emphasis on social activities and classes of interest to older people. To date, Prime Time members represent 3 per cent of their overall membership. Word of mouth seems to be an important factor in encouraging new members to join. Prime Time members tend to retain their membership longer and spend more time in the clubs with the associated possibility of spending more money. LA Fitness reports that the presence of older people has significantly increased the off-peak usage of the gym facilities.

Boys' toys

Hornby, the manufacturer of model trains, is currently undergoing a period of vigorous growth. Moving its development and manufacturing to China enabled it to cut its costs and reduce development times. Now, with a much wider range of locomotives, it is able to cater for all markets, from the youngsters buying the latest Virgin and Harry Potter train sets to older customers buying models of steam locomotives from their heyday as train spotters. In fact, many of Hornby's best customers are reputed to be middle-aged men, who now have the time and money to spend indulging their boyhood hobby. Hornby's chief executive describes this as the 'Harley-Davidson factor' – the same urge some older men have to buy the expensive motor-bikes they were not able to afford in their 20s. The median age of buyers of Harley-Davidson bikes is now 46 years, having risen from 34 in 1987. A typical Harley-Davidson bike retails in the UK for around £14,000.

Entertainment and Internet use

Audience research figures show that older people watch more hours of television a day than any other age group of the population, especially daytime television. This is well understood by programme makers (see the section 'Work and play' in Chapter 4) and advertising agencies (see the section 'Advertising' in Chapter 9).

Use of the Internet by older people is also higher than any other age group, and is still growing in terms of the number of people using it. Older people tend to use the Internet more for activities such as emailing family and friends in the UK and overseas, searching websites for information matching their hobbies or interests and researching/booking holidays and days out, rather than managing their bank accounts or paying bills. (Internet use is described further in the section 'Information and communication technologies' later in this chapter.)

The Odeon cinema group runs a popular scheme called Senior Screen for the over-50s. Showings of films, chosen by request from the often regular customers, usually take place on one weekday morning a week in most of its 59 cinemas in the UK. As well as a reduced price, customers get a free drink and refreshment, and in some cinemas staff are available to help customers locate their seats. In at least one cinema, the sound level has been turned down, and in another the range of free drinks and refreshments was changed from the usual fizzy drinks and popcorn to a hot drink and a muffin.

Tourism and holidays

Tourism is the world's biggest business and is increasingly an ageless commodity. For some people over 50, retirement is the opportunity to indulge in the travel they could not afford when they were younger; others have always travelled and don't intend stopping yet. For those who have retired, the annual holiday may well be something planned with care and anticipated for a long time in advance. There are very few things that today's older people don't do until severely limited by one or more impairments, and holidays have a high priority.

For the travel industry, tapping into this lucrative group has meant a radical adjustment from previous marketing attitudes that lumped anyone over 60 into a grey basket of frailty and inactivity. A few years ago, the perception was that older holiday-makers were content to watch the world go by from the window of an air-conditioned bus. Now the market is beginning to recognise that 'not all people over 65 want to sit in a coach with 30 other seniors and two 20-year-old guides'. People want to get out and experience the world for themselves, spending the money they have accumulated during a lifetime of work before it is too late to enjoy it. Nowadays it is not unknown for a group of people in their 80s to go on a fly–drive trip to South Africa, or for a 92-year-old to take a flying safari trip along Namibia's Skeleton Coast. There is even the suggestion that the older age groups are taking more active holidays than the younger age groups, who seem more content to chill out on the beach somewhere.

Cruising has long been a favourite holiday for older people. Some 70 per cent of cruise ship passengers are 'seniors'. The average age of cruise passengers is around 55 years, having dropped slightly in the past few years because of the attempts by the industry to attract more younger passengers. For some cruise ships, the average age may be as old as 72. Repeat business is reported to be an important factor in the sale of cruise holidays, especially to older holiday-makers. Cruising is still booming – the number of UK passengers taking a cruise holiday has more than quadrupled since 1990 and, unlike air travel, was not greatly affected by the events of 11 September. The *Queen Mary 2*, which started service in early 2004, was only the first cruise liner to enter service that year to cope with the still growing demand for ocean cruises. Another sixteen liners were scheduled to enter service during 2004 and 2005. Cruising is no longer confined to the wealthy or the able-bodied. With the advent of a variety of technological aids, disabled older travellers now have more opportunities than ever before to see the world from the comfort of a luxury cruise liner. One Florida-based company organises oxygen availability and the rental of wheelchair-accessible vehicles. It even offers 'dialysis cruises' using new, portable dialysis equipment aboard a number of cruise ships. Registered nurses and nephrologists are in attendance on board so that people can receive treatment exactly as they would at home.

Some smaller cruise lines specialise in attracting up-market passengers whose average age is in the late 60s by operating educational and cultural itineraries in exotic destinations around the world. Older travellers are also fuelling a growing field of 'study travel', sponsored by professional organisations, zoos, universities and similar institutions.

Whilst there has been a growth in the number of overseas and more exotic holidays by people over 50, the statistics reveal that, as people progress through their Third Age towards the Fourth, an increasing number of them take their holidays in the UK. This and the interest of older people in the nation's heritage (the average age of a National Trust member is believed to be over 50) means that there are plenty of business opportunities arising from older people holidaying in the UK. Many older people still enjoy the freedom provided by caravanning. The average age of members of the Caravan Club is around 55, with membership typically lasting for just under ten years on average.

The saga of Saga

A section dealing with the leisure market would not be complete without charting the success of Saga, even though the majority of its profits now comes from business interests other than holidays and travel. Saga was founded in 1951 from a single hotel in Folkestone by Sidney de Haan, later known in the travel industry as 'the man who turned silver hair into gold'. Faced with the prospect of having to close his hotel during the winter months, de Haan had the idea of selling low-priced, out-of-season holidays to retired people. They would be offered all-inclusive holidays, with coach travel and full board. The travel agents were not interested in the idea, so de Haan marketed the idea himself. He calculated that Yorkshire and Durham were the travel limits for coach travel to Kent and so targeted retired miners and steel workers and their families in those areas. The idea took off rapidly. Mr de Haan bought another hotel, and other towns on the south coast wanted to take part in the off-season hotel business. From these beginnings Saga has grown into a major holiday enterprise, offering a wide range of holidays, including short breaks, long-haul travel, safari trips and activity holidays. The organisation has also cashed in on the growing cruise business, owning at least one cruise ship itself.

From small beginnings, the Saga Group has grown to an annual turnover of £383 million (2003/4), with pre-tax profits of £81 million – an increase of 62 per cent over the previous year. It now employs over 2,500 people, mostly in the Folkestone and Ramsgate area. However, around 80 per cent of the profits comes from business interests outside travel and holidays. In the early 1980s the group started to diversify its business and address the over-50s market. Products such as home insurance, car purchase and insurance, and financial services have been now been added to the portfolio. Attracting people over 50 to a well-established brand largely associated with those over 65 required careful repositioning in the marketplace. The organisation also launched *Saga Magazine*, now Britain's second best-selling monthly subscription magazine whose readership has supplemented Saga's already substantial customer database. This database of some 8 million entries and 2 million active customers is a valuable business asset for the group, as it can be used to cross-sell products from one customer segment to another, exploiting Saga's brand image and reputation for good service. More recently, it has strengthened its media interests: Saga now owns five radio stations – two on national digital radio and two fm stations in the West Midlands, plus the franchise for a new fm station in Glasgow. These stations mainly broadcast music from the 1940s, '50s and '60s, together with items of interest to people over 50. Like many of their other business ventures, these radio stations are proving very popular with their intended audience, the growth in their listening figures bucking the current downward trend in radio listening.

However, you do not have to be the size of Saga to be successful in the leisure business. Take the case of the Royal Cumberland Hotel in Blackpool. It was not a flourishing business when taken over a few years ago by its joint owner, Vaughan Kennedy. Modernising the hotel, fitting a lift, tasteful decoration and careful publicity were the keys to building a flourishing hotel business aimed at older visitors. He has consistently achieved his business targets ahead of schedule and claims a high repeat business for customers, the majority of whom are older people. The hotel has also won the Blackpool Hotel of the Year on two occasions. Unlike Saga, however, there is nothing on the hotel website or in the hotel publicity material to indicate that the hotel is intended for (or restricted to) older people. Indeed, the lift that was so essential for older guests to reach the higher floors is advertised as a distinctive feature of the hotel to attract all guests ('the only hotel in Blackpool with an exterior scenic lift').

Implications

The leisure sector of the economy is one that has already been successful in generating business from older people. Furthermore, this business is still growing, not least because of the increasing diversity of interests of older people and their improving financial situation. Important factors for success in this sector are careful marketing and positioning of the products on offer. Selling on lifestyle is more successful than selling on age unless age can be used to make people over 50 an attractive financial offer. Saga in particular has built its brand on developing a good understanding of the needs of its customers so that it can provide them with a high-quality service, creating an image of a company that can be trusted. This lesson can be applied in any business sector of the mature market.

Information and communication technologies

Older people as technology users

This section looks at the market for products based on information and communication technologies (ICTs). In discussing older users, we need to make the important distinction between today's older people, many of whom have not experienced high-technology products during their working lives, and tomorrow's older people for whom the technology is already an integral part of their lives. The latter group are unlikely to stop using ICT products when they get older, and so it is primarily older people coming new to the technology whom we consider here.

Many studies have revealed that today's older people have become competent users of high-technology products where they perceive that those products deliver something of value to them. For example, older people have taken to texting on mobile phones where it helps them keep in touch with their grandchildren. Although people may initially find difficulty in using software, such as word-processing packages, the underlying technology is really quite forgiving; typing errors are so easy to correct! As a consequence, many more people, older ones included, have learnt how to produce nicely typed letters and documents than would have been the case had they had to use typewriters. Research also shows that, although older people might be slower at completing tasks than their younger counterparts, they are ultimately just as capable in their use of the technology. Currently, people over 50 are the fastest growing group of Internet users in the UK and, as a group, they spend more time on-line than any other age group of the population.

A survey in 2002 commissioned by Age Concern and Barclays revealed that two-thirds of IT users in the 55+ age group agreed that the Internet had had a positive impact on their lives. Most of them had used the Internet for contacting friends and family in the UK or overseas and for searching websites for information of personal interest. Banking and Internet shopping were less popular. Patterns of use varied across the UK. However, there were still many people aged 55+ who had never tried the Internet, and 66 per cent of older non-users said they had no intention of ever taking part in the IT revolution. This negative attitude is of some concern if the nation is to avoid a digital divide between the IT-literate and non-literate at a time when national and local government and commercial organisations are putting more of their services on-line. Furthermore, as we described in the previous chapter, use of the Internet may increase an older person's ability to remain longer in their own home through access to formal and informal caring services. The increasing importance of the technology is likely to continue as wireless communication at personal and household device level continues to grow, enabling communication to take place anywhere.

To prevent older people from falling the wrong side of the digital divide, Age Concern has developed a range of national initiatives, some in conjunction with external partners, to increase the availability and take-up of computers and the Internet as a means of delivering services, conquering isolation, empowering individuals and bringing together people with shared interests. Computer Explorer buses have toured the country and a number of local Age Concerns have set up computer taster sessions where older people can get one-on-one assistance with learning how to use computers and the Internet. These have proved to be very popular. Another example of computer training for older people is Hairnet, set up in 1997 to provide computer and Internet training for people over 50. This proved to be very successful and Hairnet has now moved to a new business model managing a network of older self-employed computer trainers across the UK, providing one-to-one training for people of all ages. Hairnet also organises the annual Silver Surfers Day in May, intended to raise awareness of Internet surfing for people over 50, with local taster and training sessions across the UK.

Hardware, software and information content

BT's Big Button phone is an example of a highly successful inclusively designed communication product. The phone was designed in close co-operation with two major charities, the RNIB (Royal National Institute of the Blind) and RNID (Royal National Institute for Deaf People), to meet the needs of sight-, hearing- and dexterity-impaired users, hence the choice of large buttons and an adjustable volume control. To avoid any stigma associated with the use of such a phone, the design intentionally appealed to design-conscious users as an easy-to-use corded mainstream phone. On product launch, the phone was an immediate success, becoming BT's fourth best-selling phone within a month. The business targets for the first 18 months were met within four months.

Specialist hardware peripheral devices are now available to help older or disabled people access computers. Most of these are easily integrated into the operating system of a personal computer. They are primarily alternative input devices such as special keyboards for people with dexterity problems or mouse replacements such as tracker balls or joysticks.

Much of the functionality of many products, not just IT products, is provided today in software. It may be embedded, as in the computer-controlled engine-management systems of the modern car where it is invisible to the user, or it may be highly visible in the applications that people use direct, such as email, word processing or mobile phones. Many of the more powerful accessibility features on computers are provided by software such as speech recognition and synthesis, optical character recognition (OCR) and features that enable text to be selectively magnified on a screen. So a computer equipped with a scanner, OCR and a speech synthesiser enables a blind person to read books or typed letters. Microsoft's accessibility website now includes a section specifically on ageing and the implications of changing demographics on the use of IT in the workplace (www.microsoft.com/enable/aging/default.aspx).

Interestingly, the link from the main accessibility page is entitled Baby Boomers and not Aging!

There is also a growing range of application software that caters for a huge diversity of games, entertainment, education and leisure activity that stimulate the mind and retain interests. In a leisure context, this means that people can 'experience' outdoor pursuits they can no longer physically pursue through the medium of a computer screen, keyboard and games paddles. For example, one group of older men meets regularly in their community centre equipped with computers to use the flight simulators to relive the Battle of Britain. Over all, however, older people play games on computers much less frequently than their grandchildren.

The design of websites is primarily about creating effective human communication, rather than being a matter of technology. Given that many companies and organisations now use Internet technology to communicate with employees, customers and the general public, we need to consider information content here. Even if the primary hardware and software components are made accessible to older people, it is vital that the information content is also made accessible, irrespective of whether the site is concerned with shopping, government information and services or leisure information. As often happens with a new, yet-to-mature technology, websites vary hugely in their ability to communicate information and the ease with which users can find the information they want. There are many guides to help people design websites that are accessible and easy to use, but still the design of many sites fails to follow these guidelines. For example, see the two websites listed at the end of the 'Further reading' for this section.

For older users, especially those not familiar with the technology, websites need to be designed to be easy to navigate and based on the users' requirements as to what they might want to do, instead of reflecting the (irrelevant) structure of the website itself. In fact, in a well-designed website, it should not be necessary for the user to look at the web structure to find what they want – they should be able to navigate it easily using the facilities provided.

People designing websites to be accessible are not without help, however, as services are available to enable websites to be assessed by experts who understand the requirements of different user groups. The charities RNIB and AbilityNet are two examples from the voluntary sector; both employ the web accessibility guidelines issued by W3C, the standards body governing operation of the Internet. AbilityNet produces a quarterly series of reports on websites in different business sectors. The first three covered airlines, electronic newspapers and banking. Most websites failed dramatically to meet the accepted guidelines. On a star rating system of one star (inaccessible) to five stars (very accessible), none of the airline or electronic newspaper sites reviewed met the most basic levels of accessibility (three stars), with the airline sites scoring slightly better than the newspaper sites. Over all, the bank sites performed better than the others, one of them meeting the minimum accessibility criteria (three stars). These accessibility criteria define what is required to facilitate access for users with a vision impairment, dyslexia or a physical disability that makes a mouse difficult to use. Under the Disability Discrimination Act, it is illegal to bar disabled users from using on-line services offered to the general public.

At the other extreme, the Tesco website contains an Access site (www.tesco.com/access), awarded four stars, specifically designed to make on-line shopping easier for disabled people. Designed with the assistance of the RNIB, it is entirely text-based and simple to navigate. It is also popular with people without impairments because of its clean design and ease of navigation. The Access site is reported to have been responsible for generating an additional 25,000 on-line customers.

The future

The Broadcasting Act of 1996, governing the establishment of digital television services in the UK, mandated that up to 10 per cent of digital television programmes should, within ten years, have audio description (an accompanying spoken commentary) to help visually impaired people. However, no requirements were put in place as regards access to electronic information. A recent report prepared for the Department of Trade and Industry estimated that over 25 per cent of the population aged between 65 and 74 would have some difficulty in installing a set-top box unaided, rising to almost 50 per cent for those 75 and over. The basic television facilities, such as switching to the right channel, were also found to be more difficult than with current analogue TVs. A particularly bad example of usability for one set-top box was that access to the subtitle features required the viewer to navigate down three levels of menu in order to reach them. This is difficult for people not used to hierarchic menus on computers, particularly older people who have never used computers. Compare this with four or five button presses on an analogue television (to reach Ceefax page 888). It seems as if the lessons about the poor usability of video recorders have not been learnt by those in a hurry to design our next generation of domestic TV equipment.

In the information age, access to services will be increasingly mediated by information and communication technologies, virtual travel taking the place of, or augmenting, real travel. Already shopping, money management, accessing government information and benefits are all possible without setting foot outside your door. Other services, such as access to a doctor or electronic voting will surely follow in due course. As the requirements of older people are no different from the rest of the population, it is vital that new services are designed in such a way as to make them easy to use by all sectors of the population, not just the IT-literate or the able-bodied. This is the inclusive design approach we described in Chapter 6. Help is available from a large number of sources to those designing new services to make them accessible to older people and those with disabilities, but is frequently ignored.

Further reading

Age Concern, Barclays and ICM. (2002). *IT, The Internet and Older People* (see www.icmresearch.co.uk/reviews/2002/it-internet-old-people.htm)

Gill, J. (2004) *Access-Ability: making technology more useable by people with disabilities*. London: RNIB (see also www.tiresias.org/guidelines)

Keates, S. and Clarkson, J.P. (2003) *Countering Design Exclusion: an introduction to inclusive design*. London: Springer-Verlag

Klein, J. (2004) *Researching the Transition from Analogue to Digital Television for UK DTI* (see www.fp.rdg.ac.uk/equal/Methodology/Jeremy_Klein2.pdf)

Microsoft: www.microsoft.com/enable/aging/default.aspx

Moulton, G., Huyler, L., Hertz, J. and Levenson, M. (2002) *Accessible Technologies in Today's Business*. Redmond CA: Microsoft Press International

www.20plus30.com/marketing/pdf/good_bad_ugly.PDF [for a review of government web sites from an older user's perspective]

www.academyinternet.com/consulting/Making%20The%20Web%2050+%20Friendly.pdf [for advice on web design for older people]

Housing ● ● ● ● ● ● ● ● ● ● ● ● ● ● ●

As we have argued throughout this book, the behaviour patterns of older people are very diverse, and this is no less true in the ways in which they satisfy their housing needs. Mainstream housing comes in a variety of forms, encompassing different kinds of tenure as well as different sizes and types of housing, such as the two-storey house, apartment, bungalow. However, for older people, there are additional choices of housing to match their specific needs. These include retirement communities, sheltered and very sheltered accommodation, as well as care homes (with or without nursing) for those unable to live independently. The last two categories of accommodation are somewhat different from the other choices, in that the older person is no longer living 'behind their own front door', and we do not consider them further here.

Housing is a complex subject, given its links to health, social services, amenities, planning and government policy, yet it is of enormous importance to all of us, including older people. Here we can do no more than summarise the key points as they seem to us, starting with an overview of housing needs and then considering developments in mainstream and sheltered housing.

Changing housing needs

Patterns of housing use have changed considerably in Britain over the past 50 years. In the 1950s, most older people lived in rented accommodation provided by local authorities. Today most live in owner-occupied houses and the trend toward owner-occupation is set to continue. Like the rest of the population, most older people live in mainstream housing, with less than 10 per cent of people of pensionable age living in special settings (sheltered housing, care homes etc). For people over the age of 85, however, around 25 per cent live in some form of care home. In 2000, the Royal Commission on Long Term Care investigated the options for caring for older people and showed that the cost of caring for older people in their own homes (domiciliary care) was usually the least expensive option in terms of cost to the state. This fits with the strong preference of the majority of older people for living 'behind their own front door'. The growing numbers of older people are likely to place greater demands upon social services for domiciliary care, resulting in a market opportunity to create alternative forms of housing for older people and ways of supporting them.

Another changing pattern is that of household occupancy, where there has been significant growth over the past 30 years in the number of one-person households and of households headed by a lone parent. The proportion of people aged 65 and over living alone has remained stable since the mid-1980s, however. Whether it will do so in the light of the increased numbers of younger people living alone remains to be seen. Currently, 60 per cent of women over 75 live alone, compared with 30 per cent of men, due mainly to women living longer than men and tending to marry older husbands. Much of a local authority's social care budget goes towards supporting older women living alone. The 2001 Census shows as national averages 14 per cent of households occupied by a single pensioner, with another 8.5 per cent by a pensioner family. These proportions vary considerably across the UK, with places such as parts of the south coast of England and the north Norfolk coast having a much higher proportion of pensioner households.

Not surprisingly, the condition of the existing housing stock also varies considerably across the UK, houses that have been built more recently generally being in a better condition than those built earlier. However, much of the new town stock built in the 1940s and 1950s has reached the stage where serious modernisation is required. This will be difficult for poorer older people to afford and so there is the real risk of owner-occupier accommodation becoming increasingly unsuitable for these occupants. Releasing money tied up in the value of their homes is one way of alleviating this problem and is the rationale for equity-release schemes that we discuss later in this chapter. People living in rented accommodation owned by registered social landlords are more likely to have their accommodation kept in good condition, including minimising the risk of accidents. For older people, most accidents occur at home; hence poorly equipped and maintained homes are a major source of mobility-threatening accidents.

For the working population, employment is a major factor determining where they live, and the consequences of large developments in the past are clear today in the demographics. For example, post-war new towns such as Stevenage and Harlow, built around 50 years ago, are projected to show significant rises in the number of people over 85 in the next few years. Most people grow older in places where they have lived for a number of years, and older people are the least likely age group of the population to move. Indeed, 44 per cent of the population still live in the local authority within which they were born.

For the foreseeable future, most older people will be living in mainstream housing. For those who are fit and able, there are few problems, and the mental and physical challenges of managing one's own home and garden can provide useful stimulation and activity. However, as people become frail the mental and physical effort of maintaining one's own home becomes more difficult and sometimes overwhelming. In Chapter 7, we looked at some technological possibilities that would help people to carry on living behind their own front door for as long as possible. However, we pointed out that technology is only a partial solution. Moreover, it is unlikely that we will ever return to the days when most older people were living close to their relatives who could provide the necessary care, so alternative solutions need to be found to the problems of increasing frailty as people age.

Older people living in their own homes may need help with such activities as housework, cooking, shopping, home decorating and repairs, garden maintenance and transport for those not able to drive. It is not only people living in rural areas who can become isolated because of poor public transport, as in many urban areas the shops may be too far away for older people to walk to them. Social services provide help with some but by no means all of these needs. Where they don't employ the staff themselves, the support is subcontracted to private care agencies or charities. Charities such as Care and Repair provide services outside the remit of social services to poorer old people. There are also schemes whereby older people with large homes rent out part of their homes at a reduced rate to young people, who in return provide some services around the house. As discussed in Chapter 10, we believe there may be scope for some interesting 'third-age business' initiatives that could provide useful services to older people in their own homes – a combination of part voluntary, part paid activities by Third Agers paid for by older Third Age clients.

Mainstream housing standards

In the early 1990s, the Joseph Rowntree Foundation defined a set of design principles that would make housing better for people with disabilities, embedded in a concept called Lifetime Homes. They argued that, if houses were built to these standards, converting a house so that it was suitable for an older or disabled person would at least be possible and at best unnecessary. Such housing would suit people at different stages of their life, so reducing the need to have to move house at a difficult time, such as when their physical, sensory or cognitive capabilities deteriorated. Where modification was needed in such homes, the costs would be less than otherwise. If the changes were incorporated into the design at the outset, they would not add significantly to the cost of the accommodation. For example, only minor additional costs are incurred in fitting a wide door rather than a narrow one, or placing electrical fittings where they can be reached without bending down. These principles influenced Part M of the Building Regulations issued in 1999, although these Regulations are mainly concerned with the visitability of the house and not its intrinsic liveability. Professional opinion is divided on how successful these Regulations have been in changing attitudes and building practice. In March 2004, the Government announced that there would be a new review of the Building Regulations, to include Lifetime Homes principles. It is possible that the principles themselves may get updated as part of the review process.

There are two opposing views of Lifetime Homes. The strategic planning perspective is that designing houses so that they can accommodate people's changing requirements as they grow older makes long-term economic sense: spend a little now and save more in the future. The Joseph Rowntree Foundation calculated that building Lifetime Homes would save the nation over £5 billion over 60 years, from reduced costs involved in housing modifications. On the other hand, some local authority housing-allocation managers feel that Lifetime Homes might encourage people to stay longer in the same (larger) accommodation, thereby preventing them from offering the homes to people with families. Builders are reluctant to build to Lifetime Homes' standards because they're not required to build them, customers are not asking for them and they are more costly. Given the certainty of an ageing population, the strategic rationale for Lifetime Homes arguably deserves further consideration, especially in areas of the south-east of England where large numbers of houses are to be built over the next 20 years.

Special-purpose housing

The previous paragraphs have addressed how mainstream housing could be made more suitable for older people, in terms of both new build and the renovation of the existing stock. The other side of the coin is the opportunity for specialised accommodation for older people – retirement communities and sheltered accommodation.

Retirement communities are relatively uncommon in Britain. A recent example is Hartrigg Oaks in Yorkshire, opened by the Joseph Rowntree Housing Trust in 1998, comprising 152 bungalows built to Lifetime Homes' standards. The buildings are clustered round a central complex of communal amenities, including a café, restaurant, arts and craft rooms, and a library. Various levels of care are available, according to the needs of individuals, and a 42-bed residential care unit is also located on site. The community is self-financing, the residents paying separate residence and community fees. Very high levels of resident satisfaction are reported. A similar development is under way at Denham Garden Village, where the Anchor Trust is modernising the former Licensed Victuallers National Homes built in the 1950s, including the extensive provision of a networked high technology environment, as described in Chapter 7. Both of these developments provide a mixture of sheltered and very-sheltered accommodation. In very-sheltered accommodation, enhanced personal and social care is available on a 24/7 basis if needed. In sheltered accommodation, the residents are expected to look after themselves, although a warden is usually available.

Most *sheltered accommodation*, however, is owned by local authorities, with registered social landlords (RSLs) more recently playing a significant role. Whilst the RSLs are setting high standards for new and renovated sheltered housing, much of the older sheltered accommodation is of poor quality by today's standards and can prove hard to let. As a consequence, there is a growing market in the development of privately owned, high-quality sheltered accommodation or retirement homes. Companies such as McCarthy & Stone are already exploiting this market opportunity. In 2002/3 this firm reported a market share of

60 per cent of the booming retirement-home market, pre-tax profits having risen from £28 million to £116 million in five years. Their operating margin of 42 per cent, which had also grown over this period, was significantly ahead of that of companies in the mainstream house-building sector. The retirement sector of the housing market is relatively profitable because of the increased demand for this type of accommodation by people who are mostly downsizing from larger properties and therefore have money to spend.

Implications

There is growing acknowledgement that flexibility, choice, independence, information and involvement are the key issues for today's older people in relation to the accommodation and housing services that they receive. The one-size-fits-all policy of 30 years ago is no longer relevant. Companies focused on older people, such as McCarthy & Stone, have shown that it is posssible to run a very profitable business building and running retirement homes. Given that the majority of older people will continue to live in mainstream housing, is it possible to identify attractive opportunities for providing some of the retirement home features and services for people who choose to live in mainstream accommodation? Gardening, decorating and home maintenance are obvious examples but are there others? What might the financial basis for these services be – commercial, voluntary or a combination? We outline a possible financial model in Chapter 10.

Further reading

Appleton, N.J.W. (2002) *Planning for the Majority: the needs and aspirations of older people in general housing*. London: Joseph Rowntree Foundation (www.jrf.org.uk/bookshop/eBooks/ 1842630970.pdf)

Croucher, K., Pleace, N. and Bevan, M. (2003) *Living at Hartrigg Oaks: residents' views of the UK's first continuing care retirement community*. London: Joseph Rowntree Foundation (www.jrf.org.uk/bookshop/eBooks/1859351336.pdf)

Hanson, J. (2001) 'From "special needs" to "lifestyle choices": articulating the demand for "third age" housing', in: S. Peace and M. Holland (eds) *Inclusive Housing in an Ageing Society*. Bristol: Policy Press

Imrie, R. (2003) *The Impact of Part M on the Design of New Housing* (www.gg.rhul.ac.uk/jrf.pdf)

Office of the Deputy Prime Minister. (2003) *Preparing Older People's Strategies: linking housing to health, social care and other local strategies*. London: Office of the Deputy Prime Minister (www.housing.odpm.gov.uk/stellent/groups/odpm_housing/documents/page/odpm_house_609052.pdf)

Rolfe, S., Leather, P., Mackintosh, P., et al. (1993) *Available Options: the constraints facing older people in meeting housing and care needs*. Oxford: Anchor Housing Trust

Tinker, A., Wright, F., McCreadie, C., et al. (1999) 'Alternative models of care for older people', in: *Research*, volume 2 to *The Royal Commission on Long Term Care*, London: The Stationery Office (www.archive.official-documents.co.uk/document/cm41/4192/4192-2v2.htm)

Transport ● ● ● ● ● ● ● ● ● ● ● ● ● ● ● ●

Transport provides the means for older people to keep in touch with friends, family and the wider community, and to get access to facilities and services. Accessible transport is vital for ensuring independence and autonomy. A lack of mobility can lead to low morale, depression and loneliness. In particular, there is evidence that having to cease driving is associated with increased depressive symptoms.

For retired people the main purposes of travel are to visit the shops, entertainment, participation in social interaction and community activities. The benefits of travel do not arise solely from what happens at the destination of the journey. There are also psychological benefits from getting out and about and from the casual encounters with acquaintances, as well as health benefits from walking and cycling.

Older people are time-rich. Nevertheless, travel diminishes with increasing age – although older people are travelling greater distances than in the past, as indeed is everyone. Men in their 50s make 1,200 journeys per year on average, declining to 800 by their late 70s; for women the figures are a little lower at 1,000 and 600 respectively.

Access to a car is the single most important factor affecting travel by older people. Of men in their 50s, 85 per cent are drivers in households with a car, falling to 60 per cent for those in their 70s. For women the figures are lower – 60 per cent and 25 per cent respectively. Currently there are more than 2 million people aged 70 and above who hold a driving licence. Over next 15 years this number is likely to more than double, to 4.5 million, a result of both the ageing of the population and the fact that around three-quarters of the present cohort of mid-life women hold a licence, compared with less than half of their mothers' generation.

Regular drivers aim to continue for as long as possible and many dread the prospect of having to give up. Nevertheless, the onset of physical, sensory or cognitive impairments results in declining driving ability. This means that older motorists have to adjust their driving practices, initially avoiding high-speed roads, for instance, or tricky manoeuvres such as turning right across heavy traffic; and then perhaps ceasing to drive at night or in peak hours.

There are business opportunities to be had helping older drivers to keep going, through developments in motor vehicle design and technology. It is relevant that households headed by men aged 65–69 and women aged 60–64 are more likely to own a car of up to one year old than any other age group, probably new cars bought on retirement. Inclusive design, as discussed in Chapter 6, will promote sales to the growing numbers of older motorists, particularly if the manufacturers can overcome their inhibitions about spelling out the benefits. Current standard features such as power steering and automatic gear change assist those with modest physical disabilities. A wide range of specialist adaptations and accessories is available to aid drivers with particular disabilities, including electronic accelerator and brake systems, joystick steering, and hand controls for manual and automatic gear change, some of which might become mainstream features in time. Advances in information and telecommunications technologies are contributing to the development of what is known as 'transport telematics'; features entering the marketplace, initially at the top of the range but diffusing down over time, include navigation aids, reversing aids, assisted night vision, and intelligent cruise control which regulates the distance between vehicles.

Eventually, drivers have to give up their car, which leads to dependence on lifts from others or on public transport – which many will experience difficulty in using. In contrast, regular users of public transport plan to continue using familiar local buses and trains, benefiting from concessionary fares and rail discount cards. Inclusively designed buses with low floors benefit not only older people but also mothers with push-chairs and people with luggage, all of whom find boarding easier. The operators see these buses as commercially attractive because, although they cost more, boarding times are shorter and hence routes are traversed more efficiently, yielding economies in operating and capital costs.

For bus operators, older travellers represent a potential growth market. The concessionary fare schemes that local authorities are obliged to operate allow everyone aged 60 and over to travel at half price or less outside the morning peak time. Concessionary fares are very popular with older travellers, and one recent study found that 40 per cent of pass-holders said they make more trips than they would otherwise. Take-up rates by those eligible can be high – over 80 per cent in conurbations with extensive public transport services but falling to 30 per cent in rural areas.

Bus operators are reimbursed for revenue lost through the concessionary fare discount, after taking into account the extra travel generated. The present level of compensation to operators is not ungenerous, given that they would be likely to offer reduced fares to older people at off-peak times for commercial reasons, as do the rail operators (who receive no compensation), holiday operators and many others. Take-up rates for concessionary fare schemes have tended to fall over time, in part due to increase in car ownership. Another factor may be neglectful attitudes of bus operators in meeting the needs of their older passengers, taking the form, for instance, of unreliable services, inconsiderate driving and poorly maintained bus stops which contribute to fears for personal security. Better information about routes and timetables would help attract ex-motorists who may no longer be familiar with public transport, together with assurance of a timely return trip. The nature of a journey by public transport is that it necessarily comprises a series of links in the complete chain that links home to ultimate destination and back again. For the journey to be possible, every link must be manageable. So, for instance, an inclusively designed low floor bus is not helpful for a person with limited mobility if the bus stop is too far to walk to from their front door. Successful transport operators must manage holistically and inclusively.

For people who cannot manage public transport, there are a variety of community- and voluntary-run transport schemes, such as Dial-A-Ride which is highly valued by users but suffers from the need to book, and hence plan, journeys in advance. Some local authorities operate taxi concession schemes that provide subsidised taxis to users who pay a flat fare, the local authority paying the rest up to an agreed maximum. There is likely to be scope for taxis and private hire vehicles that specialise in meeting the needs of older people, and there may be deals to be done with local authorities and other public bodies concerned with the welfare of older people – in the health service, for instance – that would provide a regular source of business.

Further reading

Atkins, W.S. (2001) *Older People: their transport needs and requirements*, summary report. London: Department for Environment, Transport and the Regions

Metz, D. (2003) 'Transport policy for an ageing population', *Transport Reviews*, vol 23, pages 375–386

Noble, B. (2000) 'Travel characteristics of older people', in: *Transport Trends*. London: Department for Environment, Transport and the Regions

Consumer products ● ● ● ● ● ● ● ● ● ● ●

This sector encompasses a very wide range of products ranging from consumer durables, such as domestic appliances, through to the so-called 'fast-moving consumer goods' sector, comprising non-durables such as food and household items. As age alone is not the primary factor in determining patterns of household expenditure, most of the items purchased by older people are those bought by the population as a whole. In this section, we highlight some specific issues related to the consumer goods sector, with an emphasis on a mainstream approach.

In providing information for people to help them make informed choices about consumer durables, it is possible to grade products for their physical characteristics; for instance, the efficiency of a washing machine and its use of resources. The assessment of product usability is much more difficult, however, as it involves the interaction between the user and the equipment in a range of domestic situations. Independent test houses therefore usually carry out this type of assessment. One that is particularly relevant is Ricability, the trading name of the Research Institute for Consumer Affairs, a national research charity dedicated to providing independent information of value to disabled and older consumers. For over ten years Ricability has conducted research to assess mainstream consumer products for their ease of use by older people and people with disabilities. They 'consistently find currently available products with good and bad features on the same model. [Their] conclusion is that too often good accessible features are there by chance rather than design.' For example, many of the very wide range of consumer products available in high street stores – say, 20 washing machines or 100 telephones – have one or more features that are difficult to use, making them unsuitable for older people with stiff fingers and poor sight. As a consequence, their choice of what to buy may be severely restricted. Although the washing performance of today's washing machines is probably better than that of machines ten years ago, there seems to have been no corresponding improvement in their usability, especially as far as older people are concerned. As we noted in Chapter 6, many of the changes that would make a product easier to use are relatively simple to implement, especially if they are a considered part of the design and not an afterthought. The reasons why these things are not done are a theme of this book.

Lack of information is clearly not a factor. There are government publications, voluntary sector bodies and commercial consultancies in ergonomics and design, all of which may profitably be consulted about the problems older people experience in using consumer products and the potential solutions to those problems. Product safety is an issue of particular concern for older consumers, because of their slower reaction times and longer healing times after injury. Ricability publishes its testing criteria as an aid both to older consumers regarding what they should look for and to manufacturers as to what they should design for. For washing machines, the check-list includes loading and unloading, detergent, controls, programme guide, indicator lights, filter and instructions. Similar lists exist for other products.

Age Concern runs a training programme called 'Through Other Eyes' that helps design teams and customer-facing commercial departments understand the older consumer, so that they can provide products and services better attuned to their needs. Participants on the course are placed in simulated situations that enable them to experience the difficulties faced by older people. Through Other Eyes has helped a wide range of organisations in different product sectors, some of which have gone on to win awards for their products. In 1999, for example, the manufacturing and packaging company McBride received the UK Institute of Packaging Star Pack award for a new bottle concept for their Frederick Fabric Conditioner, formulated after members of their marketing and production departments had participated in a Through Other Eyes event.

In a different product area, the RNIB technical information website lists 44 features that could be added to a telephone to make a real difference to disabled people, not just the visually impaired, along with information about the likely cost implication of adding those features. The site also shows the categories of impairment that would be helped by the feature, which range from a non-slip base to the ability to attach separate keyboards for those unable to use the controls on a telephone direct. As an example, the RNIB recommends that a phone should have a dial-out buffer memory to enable users who are slow in dialling to avoid being timed-out. Generally the user taps in a number and when ready presses a send key, as used on many mobile phones. It is helpful to older people in particular to have plenty of time to read a number, press the keys and check that they have entered the correct number.

One characteristic of consumer products is that most of them are not sold direct by the manufacturer to the public. The majority are purchased via high street retailers. Therefore, in order to ensure that an inclusively designed product is brought to the attention of those who would benefit from it most, it is important that a manufacturer ensures that the right information and training is provided to retailers so that their staff know that the product is especially suitable for older people. There is unlikely to be sufficient market presence if a manufacturer relies on specialist shops for the provision of inclusive products. It is a frequent complaint of older people that not only is there a limited choice of products available to them but also a limited number of outlets where they might purchase them. So, in addition to inclusive design, there is a need to consider inclusive retailing. Consumer organisations could also assist by extending their range of testing to include the needs of older people.

By 2020, half the adults in Britain will be over 50, so an increasing proportion of all consumer goods will be purchased by this segment of the population. Most of the purchases for consumer goods are repeat purchases by their very nature, so there are important issues of brand loyalty to be considered in the design and promotion of consumer goods. We consider this in more detail in the next chapter. In the present context, the point is that the repeat purchases so desired by the supplier require strong acceptance of the product by the customer. To prosper in an ageing world, the supplier needs to provide easy-to-use products that will not be rejected by customers as they grow older. The brand needs to include, not exclude. This principle extends throughout the whole range of consumer products, from the packaging of small items to major domestic appliances. It is not too soon for suppliers to be addressing this issue, as tomorrow's purchases have already been affected by today's experiences.

Of course, the way in which products are sold to older people has to be handled carefully. From its market research, one baby food manufacturer realised that older people were buying their easy-to-digest baby foods, so they launched an easy-to-digest product range for older people. This proved to be a marketing flop, as the customers did not want to be perceived as having digestive problems; their excuse for buying baby food could have been the grandchildren! Perhaps it is not surprising that some business leaders are reported to be leaving the grey market alone as being too difficult. We wish to make the contrary point, that specialist information and advice is readily available to increase the chances of a successful product launch.

Further reading

Department of Trade and Industry. *Older Adult Data: the handbook of measurements and capabilities of the older adult: data for design safety*, DTI monograph URN 00/500. London: DTI

Diamond, R. (2003) 'Why fmcg marketers need to wake up to older consumer', *Market Leader*, Autumn (see www.20plus30.com/marketing/pdf/marketleader_fmcg_brands_ageing.pop.pdf)

Disability Rights Commission. (2003) *Inclusive Design – a report by Ricability*. Report DRC/TP/IC. Stratford upon Avon: DRC (see www.drc-gb.org/whatwedo/publicationdetails.asp?id=154&section=1)

Norman, D.A. (1998) *The Design of Everyday Things*. London: MIT Press

Ricability. *Meeting the Needs of Older and Disabled Consumers: guidelines for product design and testing*. London: Ricability (see www.ricability.org.uk/reports/report-design/guidelinesforproductdesign/contents.htm)

RNIB technical information website: www.tiresias.org/phoneability/ telephones

For examples of poor design of everyday objects see www.baddesigns.com/examples.html

Health and beauty ● ● ● ● ● ● ● ● ● ● ● ● ●

As the body ages, so we are increasingly likely to encounter the illnesses, impairments and disabilities associated with later life. The relation between ageing and ill-health has been a matter for debate. Some conditions that were once thought to be a normal part of the ageing process are now regarded as distinct disease conditions. For instance, senile dementia was once supposed to be happenstance of growing old. Now, however, this is viewed as the consequence of a group of specific chronic neurodegenerative conditions, the most common being Alzheimer's disease.

One might wonder whether all the elements of ageing, not just dementia, could be thought of as illnesses. If an illness is something that can be remedied by treatment, the question is whether ageing as a whole could be slowed or prevented if we had available a sufficient range of effective medical interventions. Certainly, there is good evidence that drugs can make an impact on the progression of age-related diseases – diseases whose frequency increases with advancing age. Heart disease is the best example. Consider, for instance, statins, a class of drugs that lower cholesterol levels. Studies reveal that, for people at risk of cardiovascular disease, statins cut the risk of heart disease and stroke by a third. Those over the age of 75 benefit from treatment as much as do people under that age. One researcher has said 'Pretty much every cardiologist I know over 50 is now taking their statin every day because the results of the studies are so convincing.'

The first statins introduced into the market are about to come off patent, so prices will fall. The UK Medicines and Healthcare Products Regulatory Agency has recently agreed to a proposal to make an out-of-patent statin available over the counter, without the need to get a doctor's prescription. We are now seeing major campaigns to market this class of drugs direct to consumers. Although the profitability of a drug is much lower once 'off-patent', there are undoubtedly commercial attractions in selling a daily preventive medication to a large segment of the population.

People over 50 tend to experience chronic illness on an increasing scale as they age. In the future this group will be encouraged to engage with their own health and become 'expert patients', thus relieving the burden on their GPs, and they will self-medicate to an increasing extent. The market for medications to treat the chronic conditions of old age is surely set to burgeon, provided that research can generate safe and efficacious drugs.

In the case of Alzheimer's disease, there are now a number of drugs available which the regulatory authorities have agreed may be prescribed with the hope of slowing progression of the condition. Thus far the benefits are fairly modest, but the prize to the pharmaceutical company that is able to develop a really effective drug is of course immense. A problem with dementia is that, once symptoms are evident, the scale of damage to the brain tissue is substantial and irreversible. So a means of early detection of the onset of the condition would be very valuable.

The general view of researchers who study the biological basis of ageing is that people would still grow old even if we could eliminate all the age-associated diseases, such as heart disease, dementia, cancer and arthritis. A key question that is attracting substantial research interest is whether a detailed understanding of the biochemical and genetic processes involved in ageing would permit us to design drugs – 'anti-ageing drugs' – that would slow down the ageing process. If this could be achieved, we could regard old age as a treatable illness. This is not the case at present, but in the future it might conceivably be. Certainly, knowledgeable biologists who study the underlying nature of ageing believe that research may one day suggest ways to slow its progression and delay the onset of infirmity. However, many of these scientists are concerned about the large number of entrepreneurs, especially in the USA, who are claiming a scientific basis for the anti-ageing products they currently recommend and often sell. In 2002, 50 scientists active in the field of ageing research stated that in their view no currently marketed intervention has yet been proved to slow, stop or reverse human ageing, and some can be downright dangerous.

If the underlying processes involved in physical and mental ageing cannot be slowed at present, what are the prospects for tackling superficial appearances? Skin care is the biggest growth area for cosmetics companies, with sales increasing at 9 per cent per annum. So-called 'anti-ageing' creams now make up more than half the skin-care market. Olay, a Procter & Gamble brand, markets Regenerist, which is said to contain an 'exclusive amino-peptide complex that beautifully regenerates cells in the skin's outer layer'. Boswelox Wrinkle de-Crease is claimed to be a 'breakthrough phyto-complex created by L'Oréal Paris that combines a power dose of *Boswellia serrata* extract and manganese, which help reduce the appearance of lines caused by facial micro-contractions'. Versions of this formulation are available for successive age groups starting at the age of 30.

Beiersdorf of Hamburg owns the Nivea brand. Five years ago it formulated a product to include co-enzyme Q10, which is claimed to protect the skin from the harmful effects of the environment, especially against free radicals that cause it to age faster. Nivea Visage Coenzyme Q10 is promoted at a premium price, four times that of plain Nivea Crème. This is an example of a brand trading up to deliver what has been termed 'mass luxury at modest retail prices' (with attractive margins), in this case by responding to the desire to stay young.

The research budgets of the cosmetics companies are proportionately only a fraction of those of the drug companies, however, so evidence of the effect of these skin treatments is not likely to be well demonstrated through controlled trials. In fact, no regulatory approval of cosmetics treatments is required unless a company claims there are changes to the skin as a result, so marketing claims tend to sidestep the question of whether there is real biological activity. Whereas a treatment for eczema, for instance, requires regulatory approval, a claim to promote healthy skin does not. This discourages cosmetics companies from seeking genuinely active ingredients or advertising their properties, for fear of having to undergo expensive trials. Nevertheless, research on skin treatments is being taken increasingly seriously by some of the major cosmetics companies.

The term 'cosmaceutical' has been coined to describe drugs that affect our appearance or cosmetics that change the structure or function of our bodies. Sales of cosmaceuticals are only a tiny fraction of pharmaceutical sales at present, but this could change if promising results found, for example, an anti-baldness drug with no side effects. Thus far, cosmaceuticals are mostly drugs developed for other purposes whose unexpected side effects have been found to benefit appearance. The first was trans-retinoic acid, the biologically active form of vitamin A, which is used to treat acne but has also been found to smooth wrinkles caused by exposure to sun. This has been approved for marketing by the US regulatory authority as an anti-ageing skin treatment and is found in numerous face creams available over the counter. Other examples include Propecia, which delays hair loss, and was originally developed as a drug to treat benign prostate tumours, and Rogaine, also for hair loss, developed to treat high blood pressure. However, potential problems with side effects, and the risk of being sued on that account, may limit the attractions of cosmaceuticals to the drug companies.

Obesity is well known to be a growing problem in our society. The main causes are ready food availability, leading to excess intake, and sedentary living. Treatments are being worked on by researchers in universities, hospitals and pharmaceutical companies, both to treat disease and to improve appearance. One, Xenical, made by Roche, is available on prescription. It seems unlikely, however, that drugs to counter obesity would be approved for over-the-counter sales because of the potential for abuse by people with eating disorders.

Obesity occurs in later life, of course, but so does malnutrition. A 1994 study found that a third of older patients were overweight on admission to hospital, and 40 per cent were under-nourished.

There is therefore a clear case for nutritional supplements – to include energy, protein, vitamins and minerals – for older people at risk of malnutrition.

Anxieties about possible deficiencies in micronutrient intake – vitamins and minerals – have led to the growth of a substantial industry devoted to the manufacture and supply of nutritional supplements. It is estimated that 30 per cent of the US population is currently taking vitamin supplements. Older people in the UK are known to be regular consumers of nutritional supplements. In one recent study, which covered 1,500 adults aged over 75 years, 43 per cent reported taking some form of nutritional supplement, the most common of which was cod liver oil taken by 25 per cent.

The need for such supplements depends on a person's dietary intake. A vitamin pill is no substitute for a healthy diet, because foods contain additional important components such as fibre and essential fatty acids. Nevertheless, many experts believe that a daily multivitamin makes sense for most adults, given the greater likelihood of benefit than harm and considering the low cost. A proviso is that the dose of each component should not exceed the officially recommended daily allowance. There are potential dangers in over-dosing, as was pointed out in a report by an expert group of the UK Food Standards Agency on safe upper limits, published in May 2003.

One consequence of the publication of this report was that the Saga Group decided to withdraw from selling nutritional supplements suited to the needs of older people. The company took the view that changing opinions being expressed by expert bodies made it increasingly difficult to provide unambiguous advice in response to the growing numbers of customers' requests for specific advice about which and how much of their products to consume.

Saga's decision is impressive, from the perspective of corporate social responsibility and ethics. At the same time, given the existing wide usage of supplements, it is arguable that the withdrawal of Saga, an ethical and reputable source, was not necessarily the best decision in terms of the interests of older people. A recent World Health Organization (WHO) review of the nutritional needs of older people finds that there is a scarcity of information concerning this group's specific nutritional requirements. It is possible that micronutrient intakes in older people may need to be higher than recommended in current WHO guidelines. It is clear that more information must be gathered about the micronutrient needs of older people, including optimal intake of micronutrients, the dietary contribution to micronutrient needs, ability to absorb, and hence the case for supplementation. Also to be addressed are the implications of the existence of safe upper limits to intake, and the advice that a reputable supplier would wish to provide its customers, both as part of the packaging and in response to enquiries from users. There is a market opportunity here to develop a trusted, ethical source of supply of vitamins and minerals tailored to the needs of older people, based on the best available laboratory and clinical evidence.

Beyond the vitamin pill, there is an ever-increasing range of fortified and functional foods with alleged health-promoting effects. These are intended to supplement the inadequate nutrition provided by a diet of junk and convenience foods. The term 'nutraceutical' is used to designate bioactive natural compounds that have health-promoting or disease-preventing properties. Regrettably, there is a dearth of good clinical trials designed to assess the benefits of such functional foods. There is, for instance, some evidence that glucosamine sulphate has beneficial effects on osteoarthritis. However, because this is based on trials with small numbers of patients, there is uncertainty about both efficacy and toxicity, and better evidence is needed from larger trials.

Generally, the medical and scientific communities remain sceptical about neutraceuticals because of concerns about the quality of the evidence and the variation in potency and purity of products from natural sources. Nevertheless, the market is buoyant, in part because products sold as dietary supplements are not required to undergo the rigorous tests of safety and effectiveness that medicines must pass before they can be sold to the public.

Consequently, these supplements come with no guarantees of purity or potency, no established guidelines on dosage and often no warnings about side effects if taken along with approved medications. The European Commission is proposing regulations that would prohibit vague claims but would allow hard claims if the evidence is solid. As in the case of micronutrients, there is an opportunity for a supplier who is prepared to become a trusted and ethical source of supply of functional foods that recognise the particular needs of older people.

Further reading

Gapper, J. (2003) 'Skin care, science and the secret of eternal profit', *Financial Times*, 21 October

Kattan, M.B. (2004) 'Health claims for functional foods', *British Medical Journal*, vol 238, pages 180–181

Olshansky, S.J., Hayflick, L. and Carnes, B.A. (2002) 'No truth to the Fountain of Youth', *Scientific American*, June, pages 78–81

Pearson, H. (2003) 'In the eye of the beholder, *Nature*, vol 424, pages 990–991

Willett, W.C. and Stampfer, M.J. (2001) 'What vitamins should I be taking, doctor?', *New England Journal of Medicine*, vol 345, pages 1819–1824

Financial services ● ● ● ● ● ● ● ● ● ● ● ●

Need for advice

People in their 50s are approaching the time when their financial, housing and pension wealth will peak, before this starts to run down following the cessation of income from employment. Those over 50 ought to be in the market for wealth-management expertise to help ensure that their resources are optimally employed, so that they can sustain their quality of life through the period of old age. However, the evidence suggests that the market is not working effectively.

It is at first sight surprising that the major banks, building societies and life insurance companies are not more successful at marketing services tailored to the needs of their older clients, about whom they have a great deal of detailed information. The availability of sophisticated customer-relationship management tools makes this deficiency even more surprising. Perhaps the explanation lies in the marked growth in competitive pressure in the financial services sector, which has resulted in big discounts being offered to attract new business, with existing customers often charged substantially higher rates for the same service. This discriminates against older customers, who see their loyalty working against them. The banks seem to be relying on inertia to retain long-standing clients. It remains to be seen how long this risky strategy will continue to succeed.

Research commissioned by the Financial Services Authority (FSA) suggests that, in general, people tend to plan actively for retirement in the last ten years before retirement; for example, by increasing the level of their pension contributions. Before then other priorities take precedence, particularly the needs of children and the mortgage. Pensions are seen as the main vehicle for providing for retirement, with little consideration given to other forms of savings. Most of the key financial decisions are taken in the period of a couple of years before retirement and the couple of years after. In the run-up to retirement, people often pay for major-expenditure items, such as buying a new car or doing up the house. Many see the need for advice and information in relation to financial matters around retirement. One decision for which advice is often sought is what to do with the lump sum from an occupational pension scheme. Employer-organised seminars are an important source of advice for many people and often a way of getting access to an adviser. In retirement, people place the main emphasis on husbanding existing resources and adjusting expenditure if necessary, but rarely actively managing their funds. People tend not to see the need for advice after retirement, as they perceive that their key decisions have already been made. Those in retirement normally consider that their accumulation of wealth has finished and tend to remain with product choices made at retirement, wishing to minimise risk and achieve a relatively certain flow of income.

The FSA is concerned that people in their 60s and 70s do not understand the choices, benefits and risks associated with specific retirement products, the range and complexity of which is increasing. In particular, there is a lack of understanding of annuities, and of equity-release mechanisms that allow people to take advantage of the value of their own homes. Levels of home ownership are high in Britain, over 70 per cent of those in their 60s owning their own home. Most people have paid off their mortgages by the time they retire, implying a large potential market for equity-release products.

The FSA considers that the 'in retirement' advice market is currently under-developed, particularly given the growth in the numbers of people over 60. There is little general advice on how to manage what is termed the 'decumulation' (the opposite of accumulation) of assets, which should take full account of the range of consumer needs through retirement and the range of financial products that might be considered. There are a number of problems in the way of providing decumulation advice. Commission-based fees may not provide sufficient incentive to advisers to offer generic information and advice, nor to build a long-term relationship with a client in the management of a declining portfolio. And consumers seem to prefer advice about specific products, rather than generic advice, to help plan for retirement. The FSA is looking into possibilities for developing a two-tier advice market, separating the cost of advice from the cost of the product. The FSA thinks there might be a market for generic advice, perhaps from a menu of options, as the cost is likely to be lower than for specific advice. Offering generic advice might provide the basis for building trust and identifying further opportunities for more specific advice. Specific advice is very important for equity release and other decumulation products, for which advisers are required to have detailed understanding and wide knowledge.

There are evidently opportunities for providing financial advice to people in retirement tailored to meet their particular needs. However, the challenges should not be under-estimated.

There is not scope in one section of a single chapter of a book dealing with the whole mature market to discuss the full range of business opportunities that might arise from meeting the needs of older people for financial services. We consider below one topic – equity release – in a little detail as a case study, to illustrate the challenges. We then note more briefly some other opportunities.

Equity release

The objective of equity release is to make available tax-free cash for older home owners who are asset-rich but cash-poor. Around half of pensioner households in Britain are pretty close to the poverty line (just above or just below), yet nearly three-quarters own their own home, usually free of mortgage. Therefore, a lot of pensioners who have assets tied up in housing but have low incomes could be interested in equity release. So far, equity-release providers have concentrated on the top end of the property market, neglecting the needs of those who have only modest amounts of equity or who are seeking to release only a small part of their capital. Moreover, there has been only limited take-up of equity-release products. Older pensioners are nervous about relinquishing their last asset. Younger pensioners may be disappointed with the terms on offer, which reflect their good prospects for life expectancy. It is hard to achieve what many would like – modest amounts of equity release, £5,000 or so, to allow house repairs or upgrading of the central heating system, for instance, to yield tangible improvement to people's quality of life. The difficulty is that, even though small sums can more confidently be released than large, small sums involve proportionately higher costs in professional fees. On the other hand, pressures on pensions and rising house prices are increasing the attractiveness of equity release, the market for which grew from £240 million in 1999 to £850 million in 2002.

There are two main kinds of equity release. The first is *mortgage based*, often known as a 'lifetime mortgage'. This involves a loan secured on the property where the interest is rolled up and added to mortgage debt, with a guarantee that the mortgage will never exceed the market value of property. The occupier retains full ownership. The rolled-up interest is repaid when the house is sold, once the occupier dies or moves into long-term care. The amount of the loan depends on age; for example, it might be 20 per cent of the property value to someone aged 60, rising to 50 per cent in their late 80s. The minimum amount of equity release is usually £10,000. Most schemes have interest rates fixed for life.

Mortgage-based equity release has been regulated by the FSA since October 2004. Nearly all recent growth in equity release has been via lifetime mortgages.

The second type of equity release mechanism is known as *home reversion*. This involves the occupier selling part or all of the home to a company or individual and continuing to live in it as tenant with lifetime rights. On the person's death, the company receives the full value of the part of property sold, including any appreciation. The cash amounts received in exchange, whether as a lump sum or an annuity, are inevitably much less than the market value of the property – usually between a third and a half – depending on how long the occupier is expected to continue living in their home. The Government has announced that home reversions plans are to be regulated by the FSA, although the start date is not decided and will depend on new legislation being enacted.

A recent review of equity release by the actuarial profession recognised that this is generally regarded as a distress purchase. Users tend to be people over the age of 70 with income a bit above the level of means-tested state benefit, owning medium-priced houses. (People receiving state benefits risk losing these if their income or capital is boosted via equity release, whilst low-priced houses mean small-scale equity release, which is hard to handle within acceptable expense margins.) Equity release could be expanded if products were made more attractive to those under 70 and could be used for smaller sums from lower value properties. There is also a need to offer value for money, as well as to overcome reluctance of home owners and their families to dispose of part of the family home. However, attitudes of the coming generations may be different. They are likely to be more financially sophisticated, and may have different attitudes towards making bequests. Future older people could well feel less obliged to leave their homes to their children if they have previously helped them with the expenses of education and first-home purchase, and may be more inclined to seek income to sustain their lifestyle while able to enjoy it.

It is necessary to overcome the image problems of equity release, dating from the bad experiences of schemes marketed in the late 1980s which have passed into folklore. Products sold then were a combination of variable-interest mortgage and an investment bond invested in equities. In the subsequent recession, interest rates rose and the value of bonds fell, and income from bonds failed to provide income to plan holders or even cover payments on the mortgage, thus risking repossession. These products were outlawed in 1990. However, nowadays plan holders report a high level of satisfaction with current equity-release schemes.

The actuaries' review concluded that there is a clear need for a service that would help older people of moderate means and with low- to medium-priced houses to supplement their income and raise capital. The market needs more providers, particularly major financial institutions with innovative products and low administration expenses, as well as comprehensive regulation overseen by the FSA and more financial advisers with training and knowledge of equity release. The actuaries estimate that there is scope for a 20-fold increase potentially possible for lifetime mortgages. Currently, more providers are entering the market, including medium-sized and large financial institutions. The market is becoming more competitive but suffers a mixed press for seeming to offer poor value for money – perhaps more perception than reality. For this market to develop its full potential, it will be important for any suggestion of mis-selling to be dealt with speedily and effectively. Consumers have to understand the risks involved, including whether there is the possibility of negative equity, the rate of increase of debt when interest is rolled up, the impact on their estate, tax and benefit implications, any restrictions on others moving into the home (eg a carer or new partner) and repair clauses.

Saga has recently introduced an equity-release product that allows a predetermined proportion of the value of the property to be drawn upon. Only £10,000 need be taken to start with, and further tranches of £5,000 can be withdrawn later without further valuation.

Other needs for financial advice

We note briefly some further opportunities for providing financial advice and services to mature clients.

Some insurance companies treat older people as high risk purely because of their age. Motor insurance is one class where this can be found. In contrast, organisations such as Age Concern, Help the Aged and Saga offer insurance designed and priced specifically with older people in mind, taking account of good experience of risks with these customers. Such insurance covers motor vehicles, home and contents, travel and motor breakdown.

The market for long-term-care insurance is little developed in Britain as yet. The cheapest option is protection insurance involving regular premiums, or a single premium up front, or a combination, but with no return if long-term care proves not to be needed. Investment-linked schemes have been marketed, involving single-premium equity-linked investment bonds from which money is drawn to pay regular insurance premiums. The bond is returned to the estate on death if long-term care is not needed. However, poor stock market performance can fail to deliver returns sufficient to pay the premiums, as a result of which sales have plummeted in recent years and providers have withdrawn from the market. At the other end of the market is an immediate-care annuity in which a lump sum purchases an annuity that pays a guaranteed income for life to cover all or part of the long-term care fees. Since October 2004, all these products are regulated by the FSA.

The market for long-term-care insurance has not so far developed much, for a number of reasons. Such insurance is seen to be expensive. It is intended to bridge the gap between a person's income and the cost of care, which means that individuals with lower incomes have a bigger gap to bridge and so must insure for a higher amount – which is then hard to afford. Moreover, the state will pay the costs of care, subject to a means test for income and capital, with the result that the motivation for insurance is to protect wealth for passing on to beneficiaries after death, rather than to avoid poverty while living.

As noted in Chapter 2, of the total of some £35 billion left each year as bequests, over £7 billion is in the form of cash. This suggests that there may be marketing opportunities for low-risk, low-commission, ready-access savings vehicles, particularly given the continued propensity of older people to save, also noted in that chapter.

Also discussed in Chapter 2 is the large number of pensioners living in low-income households who are eligible for a wide range of social security benefits. Between a quarter and a third of entitled pensioners do not claim the Pension Credit, a third do not claim Council Tax Benefit and a tenth do not claim Housing Benefit, and take-up of Attendance Allowance may only be around half of those eligible. Total unclaimed benefits in 1999/2000 were estimated as £930–£1860 million, with the average amount of Pension Credit unclaimed being £22 per week. Main barriers to take-up are lack of knowledge of entitlement, confusion about which benefits are currently received and the stigma of receiving 'hand-outs'. A number of Government initiatives and services are designed to improve take-up of benefits – prompted in part because the main criticism of a selective approach to tackling poverty in later life through means-tested benefits is that the take-up is unacceptably low. There are also initiatives managed by the voluntary sector, although these are limited by the resources that can be made available. There may therefore be scope for the development of businesses aimed at securing benefits to which pensioners are entitled. Questions that arise include whether this could be achieved on a commission basis in a manner that is both ethical and acceptable to clients, given their low incomes; and whether, alternatively, such a service might be funded by government or interested voluntary sector organisations, in effect as an outsourced service to meet their objectives.

A general need that older people have is for affordable financial advice and financial services. Because they are drawing down their wealth and are living on incomes that are normally declining in real terms, they tend to be averse to paying levels of commission for services rendered that might have been acceptable during the wealth-accumulation phase of life. The Government has been promoting an approach to saving products with commission limited to 1 per cent per annum, although the financial services industry argues that it is hard to provide specific advice to 'low-wealth' individuals within this cost ceiling. An important factor here is the relatively high incomes expected and earned by finance professionals, which ultimately are at the expense of pensioners and others reliant on investment income, whether in the form of funded occupational pensions or of dividends and interest from investments.

Might there be a business opportunity for a low-cost source of advice and service that would be expert, ethical and trusted, as well as viable as a business? Such an approach could be assisted by current developments in Internet-based systems using sophisticated financial modelling techniques. At present these are being introduced as a means to provide a low-cost assessment of a customer's financial situation and risk profile during working life, with the aim of helping them to achieve their financial goals in retirement, in part through better asset allocation. It would be a natural extension to apply this approach to asset allocation and decumulation in retirement.

Further reading

Actuarial Profession. (2001) *Report on Equity Release Mechanisms*. Oxford: Faculty & Institute of Actuaries

Financial Services Authority. (2002) *The Impact of an Ageing Population on the FSA*. London: FSA

Financial Services Authority. (2002) *Financing the Future: mind the gap*. London: FSA

Hinton C. and McGrath D. (2003) *Using Your Home as Capital*. London: Age Concern England

Voluntary sector ● ● ● ● ● ● ● ● ● ● ● ●

In this section we look at the opportunities for companies to work with the voluntary sector. Increasingly, charities are taking a much more commercial approach to generating financial support for their charitable objectives. The major national charities concerned with older people, Age Concern and Help the Aged, also operate as affinity groups organising and co-ordinating activities on behalf of older people. Consequently, they are able to negotiate favourable terms with goods and service providers, such as insurance underwriters. Most importantly, however, all voluntary sector bodies, especially the major national charities, have valuable first-hand experience of the wants and needs of older people. It makes sense, therefore, for companies thinking about the potential of the mature market to take a look at the services and products supplied by charities or by their associated trading arms. It also makes sense for the corporate sector to take advantage of the knowledge of the voluntary sector through collaboration and partnership, something most charities are very willing to do if it benefits the people they were set up to serve.

Under the terms of the charity legislation and regulation, there are strict rules governing the business activities of charities. They are allowed to carry out business activities that are in direct support of the objectives for which the charity was established (known as primary or charitable trading); for other areas of business, they usually set up separate trading subsidiaries. As long as the profits from these trading activities are transferred to the charity by deed of covenant or Gift Aid, they are not subject to corporation tax. This arms-length relationship also means that the charity's funds are not at risk if the trading subsidiary fails.

These trading activities generate substantial sums of money for their parent organisations. Help the Aged's financial statement for 2002/3 shows that they generated over £34 million of income from trading activities out of an Incoming Resources total of £74 million. In the same period, Age Concern England received over £9.5m as Gift Aid payments from trading subsidiaries, comprising approximately 25 per cent of the money available for spending on the charity. Age Concern shops generated an income of nearly £8 million in 2002/3, yielding an operating profit of almost 10 per cent.

As noted above, voluntary sector bodies have started to use more commercial methods of raising funds to support their objectives. Both Age Concern and Help the Aged offer insurance products, and Age Concern has teamed up with Powergen to sell gas and electricity. Most major national charities now provide on-line shopping as well as the more established market channels of catalogues and local franchises or outlets. Internet shopping could be particularly helpful to people who have difficulty moving about or indeed for those who do not like being rushed or pressured into making a purchase. For companies that supply products and services purchased by older people, selling through the charities represents an additional channel to market, one that has the advantage of using the brand image of the charity. If the number of customers is great enough or the characteristics of the customers warrant it, as in the case of home or motor insurance, the charity has the possibility of negotiating favourable prices for the benefit of its customers. There may well be further opportunities for enterprising companies to market their products in this way.

Most charities are willing to supply information about their client group. Sometimes the information is freely available in brochures, books and on websites. In other cases, a more formal relationship involving a straight commercial purchase or co-operation for mutual benefit is more appropriate. We look at three examples to illustrate what has been achieved.

Some charities run consultancy activities to provide information to the commercial sector. This market has no doubt been stimulated by the requirements of the Disability Discrimination Act 1995 for accessible services and environments. For example, the Royal National Institute of the Blind offers design and audit services to the business community. These include a Web Access Centre to help web designers and managers create and implement accessible websites, web assessments and audits to ensure compliance with Disability Discrimination Act guidelines, and a product design group that works with company industrial design teams. Age Concern's training programme Through Other Eyes makes people more aware of the limitations of older people (this was described in more detail in the section 'Consumer products' earlier in this chapter). Age Concern Enterprises, the trading arm of Age Concern, has recently launched a research and consultancy service offering information about the 50+ marketplace in the UK.

Corporate social responsibility is becoming a more important agenda item in the boardrooms of major companies and could capitalise on the willingness of charities to co-operate for the benefit of their clients. As we described in the earlier section 'Information and communication technology products', Age Concern and Barclays Bank co-operate on an IT literacy scheme for older people. Another example involving one company and several charities is the Here to HELP programme led by British Gas. This is a three-year programme involving seven charities– including Help the Aged, RNIB and Save the Children – which has been visiting homes in the 500 most-deprived areas in Britain since the autumn of 2003. Low-income households are being offered the chance to improve their lives through the installation of free energy-saving measures, a benefits health-check and additional quality-of-life services by the appropriate charities involved. Whilst British Gas will install the energy-saving measures, Help the Aged will install security devices and smoke alarms through its HandyVan service and offer welfare advice for older people through SeniorLine, its confidential phone service. The RNIB is providing advice on eye health and coping with low vision, as well as free items from its product catalogue. The programme costs £150 million and is jointly funded by British Gas, social housing providers and government schemes. Working closely with charities in this collaborative way enables companies to gain a first-hand understanding of the needs of particular sections of the population as well as improving their standing through enhanced corporate social responsibility.

A third method of collaboration involves joint research projects between companies, university research groups and charities. Research projects involving partners with complementary interests have become an important approach to research in recent years, both in the UK and in Europe. Indeed, the requirement of some research programmes is that the academic groups must collaborate with both potential users and exploiters of their research from the outset. EQUAL (Extending QUAlity Life) is a national research initiative designed to encourage university-based academics and researchers to become involved with quality-of-life research for the benefit of older or disabled people, and more generally to meet the challenges of the ageing population in the UK. EQUAL is a programme of the Engineering and Physical Sciences Research Council that has funded 34 separate research projects, involving 42 research teams since 1998. A requirement of the scheme is the active involvement of disabled or older users. Frequently the role of the charities is to provide access to users and information. There is also an EQUAL network open to all with an interest in the application of research to meeting the needs of older or disabled people. With the growing interest of university-based researchers in the challenges posed by an ageing population, there are increasing opportunities for business to forge fruitful research partnerships with academic experts as well as with interested charities.

A traditional area of activity of the voluntary sector, and indeed one that gives rise to its name, is the use of volunteers to provide their time and services in support of a cause. Volunteering is a major use of people's time once they have retired. One attempt at promoting this is The Experience Corps, an independent, non-profit-making company, funded by a grant-in-aid from the Home Office. It was set up to encourage people aged 50–65 to offer their skills and experience to benefit others in their local communities. However, like many organisations trying to use these untapped resources, they have found it hard to attract people into the large number of voluntary activities available, with the result that future government support will be reduced.

However, whilst there is mutual advantage in closer links between the corporate and voluntary sectors, we must sound a word of caution. The ethos of the voluntary sector is very different from that of the corporate sector, especially at the working level where much of the effort is provided by people in their own time. The personal motivating factors of volunteers are often very different from those of employees. This factor can cause tensions even within voluntary organisations between its employees and the volunteers. Any business entering a partnership agreement with a charity should bear carefully in mind possible conflicts of ethos.

Further reading

The Experience Corps: www.experiencecorps.co.uk

9 Mature marketing

In this chapter we consider some of the practicalities of marketing to mature consumers. What can be said with confidence is rather limited, however. This is due in part to the nature of marketing as a discipline – an art as much as a science – and in part to the dearth of evidence about the behaviour of mature consumers.

We proceed by first reviewing what is known about advertising and branding, as applied to older consumers. We then consider sources of marketing expertise. And, lastly, we discuss what we must know if the wants and needs of older consumers are to be met profitably by businesses attuned to this growing market sector. The context, of course, is that the mature market is the one growth sector, the result of demographic changes.

Advertising

Older people have substantial income and wealth, and represent a major part of the market for consumer goods and services. The over-50s are reported to purchase 80 per cent of all top-of-the-range cars, 50 per cent of all face-care cosmetics, 50 per cent of mineral waters, 35 per cent of total travel and 80 per cent of all cruises. Moreover, competition for the shrinking youth market is intense.

It is therefore surprising to find that older people say that advertising and marketing generally ignores them. They report a paucity of people like themselves in ads, particularly in evening television schedules. In fact, research shows that a third of television advertisements include someone over 50, and 20 per cent feature someone over 50, although this mainly reflects daytime schedules. The over-50s age group tend to feel that most ads are not intended for people like them. One study reports that 70 per cent of people over 55 feel that advertising does not reflect their life.

The proportion of over-50s' models in mainstream publications falls well below the number of over-50s in the population, whereas in publications targeted at this age group the proportion is – not surprisingly – much higher. Ads that feature older people are mainly for financial services, health and medicine, disability aids, travel and holidays.

Whilst many older consumers claim to be disenchanted with advertising, others say they are not too bothered. Hostility and indifference to advertising tend to increase with age, while favourable attitudes decline. People over 50 are more likely than those under 50 to find advertising a waste of time, to feel it only generates superfluous needs and to be annoyed by nearly all TV ads. This might in part reflect a generation effect, a consequence of differences in exposure to television when young.

The British Code of Advertising Practice bans discrimination on grounds of race, sex and disability, but not age. It states: 'Advertisements should contain nothing that is likely to cause serious or widespread offence. Particular care should be taken to avoid causing offence on the grounds of race, religion, sex, sexual orientation or disability.' It may only be a matter of time before age is included.

The lack of images of older people in advertising is part of a more general phenomenon whereby older people are under-represented on television programmes generally, including as presenters and fictional characters. Where they are depicted, they tend to be stereotyped. Older people feel that the views of their age group are ignored by media and that they are rarely portrayed in factual programmes.

There is a shortage of knowledge about the targeting of ads towards older people, and a regrettable lack of case studies showing the effectiveness and commercial payoff of marketing campaigns targeted at the mature consumer. Basic questions include whether older people identify with images of people like themselves in ads, or should images be used corresponding to people ten years younger – in the way that the images of children in advertisements for toys are rather older than the target audience? Does this depend on the product category, and is choice of media important in this context? What does seem apparent is that focus groups of older people find sizeable variations in the effectiveness of advertising targeted at older people. Negative images of older people are a big turn-off. Stereotypical attitudes are not persuasive. But some ads elicit positive responses, for instance those of some financial institutions and of the Saga Group. And of course there are practical aspects such as font design and size, and colour contrast and the avoidance of glare, that help make text easily readable. A set of fonts, known as Tiresias, has been designed by the Royal National Institute of the Blind to be legible for as many people as is reasonably possible.

However, advertising is not about representing older people but about selling products and services. In this context there is, of course, the crucial role of product information – to aid judgements about functionality and quality; to help inspire trust, confidence and reassurance; and to defuse apprehensions. So we need to be cautious in generalising from the reactions to advertisements of focus groups involving limited numbers of older people who may not be representative of the target audience. There is indeed some evidence that attitudes and responses to advertising vary across the segments of the mature market, ranging from those who actively seek out information to those who claim to avoid any commercial messages. However, research suggests that those who are most anti-advertising include those who buy into luxury, aspirational brands, which implies that these older consumers do not want to be seen as influenced by advertising, although in fact they are. This behaviour contrasts with that of younger consumers, the majority of whom admit to being influenced by advertising.

One research study that explored the attitudes of older consumers towards advertising failed to find an outpouring of dissatisfaction towards images used – it was more of a disconnection with the brands, which were perceived as using inappropriate images. Using overtly young or old people in advertising led to the same reaction. Respondents who do not recognise themselves as old fail to connect with images of older people. In the same vein they are not kidding themselves that they are young, and will reject a very youthful image. Those creative executions that used an ambiguous middle-aged image were positively accepted. More generally, it seems that, for advertising to the over-50s consumer to be effective, a rather detailed understanding of attitudes and lifestyles may be needed (as is recognised with the youth market).

A basic question about the use of advertising to gain access to the mature consumer is whether to target this particular market sector or to adopt an inclusive approach. Much depends on the nature of the product or service, as discussed in Chapters 6 and 7. A product or service designed specifically for older people would need to be marketed mainly to this client group, although the significance of family members and others purchasing on behalf of frail elders needs to be borne in mind. On the other hand, in the case of an inclusively designed product, the option is open to advertise and market inclusively or, alternatively, through a complementary set of segmented approaches.

There is some successful experience of segmented approaches to the marketing of mainstream products and services, based on customer profiles. For instance, one motor insurer offered a standard product but tailored the renewal notice to the concerns of the customer segment, as determined from customer surveys that asked what worried people most about something going wrong with their car. Policy benefits featured in the reminder notices were, for younger women, a helpline and fast support if the car broke down on the school run; while for older men it was a quick facility for help if you had locked your key in the car.

Another example of customer profiling is based on the finding that those under 50 tend to borrow money to buy a car, while those over 50 tend to pay cash. So different marketing messages can be projected to the two age ranges via media channels that reflect the different financial situations.

A third example is the reading light sold by Alex Light – a spotlight on a flexible mounting – the ads for which contain the message: 'You may already know that … by the age of forty you need over twice the light you did in your early twenties. This can double again by the time you retire.' Presumably, the manufacturer believes that this selling point would not put off younger customers, for whom the design and functionality would be the attractions.

There is some anxiety that such segmented marketing of mainstream brands risks sending conflicting messages to different audiences. Inclusive marketing avoids this, using messages of wide appeal, for instance 'enjoy life to the full', or 'what a great age to be'. It may not be desirable to show people in advertisements, rather to project a spirit of freedom and optimism, for instance.

Whatever approach may be taken, it makes good sense to advertise in media that have a high readership by older people. More than half the readers of the *Daily Mail*, *Daily Express* and *Daily Telegraph* are over the age of 50. This is often regarded as bad news for the business prospects of such papers, on the argument that circulation is bound to decline as the ageing readership gradually dies off. This might be the case if choice of newspaper was something made when young and adhered to faithfully throughout life. But a newspaper or magazine that is attractive to people over 50 could continue to renew its readership as successive cohorts pass that age. This is the model adopted by *Saga Magazine*, with over 80 per cent of the readership over 55 but with continual promotion to bring in new readers. *Saga Magazine*'s circulation is 1.2 million and growing, while the circulations of youth market magazines are dropping.

Saga Magazine is the leading example of the 'retirement press', which came on the scene in the 1970s to take advantage of the development of a wider range of lifestyles. *Yours* was originally published by Help the Aged, now by Emap, which also publishes *Choice*. *Senior Life* is published on behalf of Help the Aged, and is still aimed at 'the elderly and sometimes frail', in contrast to the other magazines which have shifted focus to the younger age range of post-50s. However, a common view among media people is that, with a few exceptions, the range of titles specifically targeting the mature market is uninspiring to advertisers, creative people and media buyers. Hence the attraction of using the general media, which of course includes television.

Magazines that attract older readers include the gardening periodicals such as *Amateur Gardening* (56 per cent of the readership over 55) and the BBC's *Gardeners' World* (45 per cent), *Reader's Digest* (48 per cent), *Country Life* (40 per cent), *The Field* (43 per cent) and *Radio Times* (42 per cent), as well as a number of women's periodicals such as *Woman's Weekly* (53 per cent), *Family Circle* (48 per cent) and *Woman and Home* (54 per cent).

People over 50 view more television than other age groups, typically in the range four to seven hours a day, and including daytime, which is less expensive for advertising than peak time. BBC research indicates that they account for nearly 40 per cent of the peak-time television audience, with a skew towards BBC 1 and 2. For this age group television is an important source of both entertainment and news, a prime vehicle for keeping in touch, and provides a strong word-of-mouth role with friends and family. For advertisers addressing mature consumers, television avoids the perceived stigma of the 50+ specialist magazines. Fragmentation of channels enables tighter, more cost-effective targeting using simple ads – known as 'infomercials' – having clarity of message (go to the shops, pick up the telephone, post a letter) at low production cost.

People over 50 are also above-average users of radio. Saga has local radio stations in both the East Midlands and the West Midlands, as well as a national digital broadcasting station, PrimeTime Radio, targeted at this audience. Saga has created its own media channels to overcome the problem of reaching the over-50s market: *Saga Magazine*, the radio stations, direct mail and a website.

Direct marketing via telesales can be effective with older people who are not in full-time employment and hence can be contacted more readily. But cold calling over the phone can cause anxiety and irritation, especially if a meal or favourite television programme is interrupted. Empathy with the potential client is therefore important, and older operatives are found to be far more successful in this regard. There is increasing use of call centres to handle responses to advertisements, and increasing confidence on the part of older people in using them. Direct marketing in print media can also be successful with older customers, with telephone numbers to contact or coupons to post, at their leisure. Logging responses to direct sales advertisements in the press or on television allows the fine tuning of the campaign in terms of design, content and size of the ad, channel on television, position in the newspaper, frequency and the like. Televised direct marketing, using ads that include a telephone number, typically prompts one call per 5,000 viewers, most responses coming in within ten minutes of transmission. This means that the responses to peak hour ads can be hard to handle at call centres, with daytime advertising as the more cost-effective alternative, spreading the marketing budget over more advertising.

Another route to direct sales is via the Internet, where people over 50 represent 25 per cent of the online population and rising. However, making a website friendly to this class of users is not simply about using a decent-sized font. Other factors to get right are language, imagery, navigation, design and functionality, all of which have to be implemented in a way that works for the target audience, not just for youthful website designers. And then the site has to be tested, refined and retested on this same audience until the point is reached where the customer is content to surf and does not click away in frustration.

Direct marketing by mail can work well with older people, for suitable products and services. For instance, Kellogg's found that sales of All-Bran breakfast cereal had been declining, with sales to women over 55 halving in seven years. The company employed direct mail to targeted lists of mature female consumers chosen to be up-market, retired, health and weight conscious, with an active lifestyle. A money-off coupon was offered to encourage trial of the product. This allowed responses to be tracked. Coupon redemption exceeded 15 per cent, which was seen as a successful promotion and which gave Kellogg's the confidence to target this group in other ways.

In the case of direct marketing by mail it is important to weed out the names of the deceased from bought-in lists because attempts to canvass the dead tend to upset their spouses and families, damaging the brand. It is also cost effective to eliminate the names of the recent deceased, using commercially available data compiled from probate records and funeral directors, as these can be purchased at a unit cost of around a third of that of a mail shot.

Branding ● ● ● ● ● ● ● ● ● ● ● ● ● ● ●

Traditional marketing thinking holds that it is always easier to persuade someone with no existing loyalties to try a brand than to get someone with established loyalties to switch brands. Hence young people, entering the market for the first time, are the better prospects. And as young people build families, they buy more. In contrast, older people are supposed to have fixed tastes, dislike new experiences, stick to familiar brands, are nervous about new technology, don't need to make fashion statements, and live in static or shrinking households. Some claim that half the people over 50 never change brands. All of which is thought to be bad news for innovation in the consumer goods market. If this is true, an ageing population may mean less scope for pure marketing and more value in existing brands; more opportunities for quality upgrades of current ideas and premium versions of experiences already enjoyed, and indeed more scope for genuine innovation to meet needs and wants.

Other marketing practitioners are sceptical of such claims for brand loyalty on the part of older consumers, and indeed argue to the contrary that they are nowadays less likely than in the past to stick to well-known brands, and that no clear difference in brand loyalty is found between older and younger consumers (although this may depend on the brand or sector). When people over 50 buy cars, they tend to go for best deal regardless of the previously owned brand. When asked, fewer than a third of people over 50 are confident that they would purchase the same make of car again. When they seek holiday destinations, they generally ring the changes, even if they stick with a familiar travel agent.

One market research study from the USA found a decline between 1975 and 2000 in the proportion of all age groups who said they try to stick to well-known brand names. For the latter year, the proportion that was brand-loyal was steady at around 60 per cent for all age groups, except that for those in their 70s the figure rose to over 70 per cent. However, one should not place too much weight on a single study of this kind.

A more nuanced perspective would be that brand loyalty on the part of mature consumers is potentially high, but their knowledge and experience mean they can be critical customers. They have the time to shop around, and they will move to quality if it is affordable and is seen to be good value for money. They may buy quality 'to see them out', as they may hope. Businesses that undervalue brand loyalty are vulnerable – for instance, those that discriminate against established customers by treating new customers preferentially, trading on inertia. Placing full value on brand loyalty is an approach that should pay dividends as the population ages. But brand loyalty is a positive attribute, distinguishable from sticking with a service through inertia, because of the hassle of switching a bank account or utility supply, for instance.

Kath Harris, a market researcher specialising in mature consumers, has put forward an interesting perspective. Affluent mature consumers, for the first time in their lives, can focus on their own needs, wants, ambitions and dreams, rather than meeting the demands of family or work, and are now free of the stresses of working life. So they may not be converging in behaviour and attitude with other segments of society. Their hopes and fears centre on health and mobility. Without health and mobility they cannot enjoy the 'long vacation' of the earlier decades of well-off retirement. On the other hand, they have a relative lack of aspiration to acquire consumer goods because, at this life stage, fulfilment rarely depends on conspicuous consumption. Activity is their generally desired goal: charity work, hobbies, DIY, education, consultancy, holidays, health and fitness, discovery. Identity is rarely played out through the conspicuous adoption of brands. Rather, preferred brands reflect functionality – tried and tested products –

as well as social status. So, for instance, mature consumers are willing to endorse supermarkets' own-label brands on grounds of quality and value.

Perhaps mature consumers are forced into more rational purchase behaviour because brands that could be aspirational for this segment do not (yet) exist. There are many brands that trade on a youthful lifestyle; for example, Nike, Sony, Levi's and Virgin. (Will the Virgin brand age as its founder gets older, and if it continues to move into businesses such as rail travel that do not have an obviously youthful image?) Saga is perhaps the only broadly focused brand at present that targets people over 50. But some brands seem age-neutral (eg John Lewis), while others attempt in their marketing to be age-inclusive (eg Gap, Burberry). Older consumers are reported to show positive awareness of newer brands such as Ikea, Microsoft and Haagen Dazs, suggesting the acceptability of quality brands that offer new experiences.

One pervasive inhibition about age-inclusive branding derives from the belief that overtly appealing to a 50+ audience could alienate younger buyers, and vice versa. Most marketing experts allow this to be a valid concern. Others say there is no real evidence. It may well depend on just how the marketing campaign is executed.

Mature market expertise

For the topics treated in earlier chapters of this book, there is a fair basis for reaching a view on the characteristics of older people, for instance, or how to design inclusively. In contrast, we are forced to conclude that it is hard to come by knowledge about the marketing to mature consumers on which reliance can be placed. To some degree, this is a difficulty with the subject of marketing generally. However, the problem does seem especially acute when addressing the likely behaviour of older consumers, because people over 50, in all their diversity, are less well understood than other segments. For instance, a popular textbook of marketing, now in its eleventh edition, says little about older consumers when discussing the principles of market segmentation. On the other hand, there are websites that highlight current developments in the mature market, in particular www.seniorheadlines.com and www.20plus30.com/marketing/blog.htm.

Market research organisations, whose business it is to publish reports on particular sectors, report on aspects of the mature market from time to time. Many of these are listed at the useful website www.marketresearch.com>demographics>age>mature. Such reports tend to be fairly expensive and seem, from what we have seen, to have been compiled by market research generalists having no special knowledge of older people. Nevertheless, these are not a bad place to look if you're starting from scratch.

A problem with using marketing and advertising agencies is that the professionals are predominantly youthful. A survey by the Institute of Practitioners in Advertising in 2001 found that 80 per cent of staff in advertising and marketing agencies were under the age of 40, while 50 per cent were under 30. Advertising agencies compete in a massively over-supplied and competitive market with high burnout rate, so the average age tends to be quite low. A similar situation applies to staff on the client side. Among major advertisers, only one in ten marketing directors was over 50, while four out of ten were under 35.

Marketing people find it natural and comfortable to work with colleagues in advertising agencies of their own age. They see marketing as a youthful activity, all about innovation and needing new people for new ideas. Marketers are in close contact with the media, who are obsessed with getting a bigger slice of the youth market. They seek the approbation of their peer group when they cultivate and project images. Inevitably there is a lack of empathy with older people, a life stage of which the youthful marketing people have no first-hand experience, and indeed from which they may resile. It is said that marketing briefs that target people over 50 tend to get the weakest team – often the youngest, paradoxically. There is thus something of a self-perpetuating estrangement between a youth-dominated advertising and marketing industry and a maturing population. It is hard for ads to deliver if the substance is not there. Younger marketers are tempted to deliver creative imagery as a substitute for substance.

It is noteworthy that career progression in marketing is very different from that in the older established professions such as law or medicine, where people rise to their peak of achievement fairly late in their working lives. Moreover, doctors every day address the health and illnesses of older people, which contrasts with the neglect of these very same clients by marketing specialists. The specialism of geriatric medicine has long been established to cater holistically for the medical needs of older people. Although 'geriatric marketing' may be a step too far in terms of image, the marketing profession could usefully rethink its own career progression in the light of population ageing. The words of Warren Buffett are apt: 'It's hard to teach a new dog old tricks.'

In the meantime, one potential solution lies in the agencies that specialise in the mature market. Some of these are listed at the end of this chapter. Seasoned marketing specialists are more likely to be found here, although by no means all the personnel are themselves mature. Agencies argue that their staffs need to be young because the staff on the client side are also young, with heads of marketing generally under the age of 40 and not necessarily on the Boards of their companies, despite marketing being a large chunk of firms' discretionary expenditure.

The specialist agencies recognise the generic barriers to engaging the mature market, in particular the lack of understanding of consumer behaviour. They may therefore have invested in proprietary market research, both quantitative and qualitative, which, they believe, yields insights with intuitive truth for their clients. Some of these specialists in the behaviour of older consumers publish in the marketing journals and magazines, and a selection of the more interesting recent articles is noted at the end of this chapter.

A further potential source of knowledge is the academic community – researchers and teachers of marketing based in the business schools, who publish their research and ideas in the academic marketing journals. However, there seems to be a bit of a gap between the academics and the practitioners in Britain, with not much in the way of cross-reference between the two – perhaps because the over-50s academic marketing literature is based overwhelmingly on US research. In the UK this is an under-researched area.

William Lazer, a respected US marketing academic, is of the view that the bulk of statements in the marketing literature are unsupported conjectures that appear to make sense but for which evidence is lacking. Some statements are in partial conflict – for instance, that mature consumers are set in their purchasing patterns and are loyal to brands, while at the same time they are more cautious in their purchases and have time to seek out value for money. Lazer argued in a 1986 article that the mature market is among the least intensively researched and understood of the market segments, with more unsupported statements and myths than others. The position is not much further advanced nearly 20 years later.

Engaging with marketers

The caution against reliance on unsupported conjectures in planning a marketing campaign is surely valid. This points to the importance of market research and to the potential of specialist agencies to provide this service. However, there are difficult questions concerning the validity of findings from survey and focus groups involving older people. Given the diversity of this segment of the population, as discussed in Chapter 4, how can we be at all confident that a limited scale of investigation (which may be all that can be afforded) will generate valid findings? Will the focus groups be representative of the target market? If not, what are the implications? Will the surveys yield statistically significant findings on which reliance can be placed? Naturally, the market researchers will offer reassurance – this is, after all, how they make their living. But as a purchaser of these services, the client will want to cut through the bull to assess what reliable knowledge can be gained about the behaviour of potential mature consumers.

Business must go on, despite all the uncertainties. Decisions have to be made in the absence of firm data. For want of anything better, we must rely on the tenuous evidence derived from partial information, limited experience, anecdote, professional judgement and common sense. With this major health warning let us proceed to draw the threads together. What follows are some reflections that may help to put you, the potential client wishing to target the mature market, in a suitable frame of mind for discussions with marketing and advertising agencies pitching to offer their services.

Given current media coverage, there will be few senior people in the corporate sector who are not at least aware of some of the implications of population ageing. But far fewer will have a clear view of how to exploit the business opportunities. Some say that the mature market is on the Agenda but not yet in the Plan. Others think that view is optimistic – clients do not see this sector as a priority; there is a reluctance to take the plunge; and brand owners are nervous about alienating younger consumers, particularly in ex-growth sectors where a 1 per cent market build is rare.

Nevertheless, the challenge for business is to provide the goods and services that facilitate and encourage active enjoyment of old age, support aspirations and changing lifestyles, and give older people a rationale for spending rather than saving their money in ways that are life enhancing. The aim is to 'add life to years, not years to life'. Or, as Mae West said, 'It's not the men in my life, but the life in my men that matters'.

There are many common assumptions or conjectures made about older consumers and how to approach them, at least a number of which are probably myths. Despite the inconclusive nature of the evidence, these assumptions are worth bearing in mind as the basis for constructively critical dialogue with mature-market experts:

- Purchasing behaviour of older consumers may be related more to health, independence and self-sufficiency than to other factors normally considered in market segmentation.

- A significant element of the buyer base for mainstream brands is now people over 50, which has implications for marketing.

- Brand loyalty on the part of older consumers is high – but their knowledge and experience mean that they can be critical customers. Although quite conservative in purchasing decisions, they have the time to research and shop around, and they will move to better quality if it is affordable.

■ Older consumers are less influenced by the economic cycle, being no longer in work and therefore not anxious about the possibility of losing their jobs. But income may reflect fluctuations in interest rates and the value of investments in equity-based savings, and longevity is uncertain, making for caution.

■ Mature consumers differ from others in their sources of information, in their ability to learn, and in their methods for accepting new products. Direct marketing can be used to target them through appropriate choice of media, monitoring responses to fine tune the campaign.

■ Mature consumers may be customers for 'nostalgia' brands and products – although the new Volkswagen Beetle and the revamped Mini seem more popular with younger than with older people.

■ Men and women may have different attitudes to new brands and innovations, although there is a lack of firm evidence. Mature women no longer live their lives mainly through their families but live for themselves and spend on themselves. Shopping may be a source of pleasure for them, rather than a chore.

■ Consumption behaviour is shaped by the existence of a spouse or partner, and their physical and psychological mobility. The purchasing behaviour of older singles is very different from that of couples. But, in any event, older people generally live in smaller households and therefore have a preference for smaller pack sizes.

■ Mature consumers are generally late adopters of technology but, although not at the forefront, may follow suit fairly rapidly – witness the high level of mobile phone ownership by people over 50 (one-third of all), the high rate of growth of Internet use, and over-50s 'early adopters' buying digital radios.

■ Past experience is not a predictor of consumer behaviour of the new generation of people over 50, who are becoming more innovative than previous generations, have more varied lifestyles and are more discriminating. High quality prompts word of mouth recommendation amongst the time-rich.

- Older consumers see themselves as still very much part of mainstream consumption, with no age cut-off in respect of consumer behaviour. (Why do pensioners go shopping on a Saturday? Because that's the day people go shopping.)

- Mature consumers do not welcome being targeted on the basis of their age, unless there are clear advantages for them. Older consumers do not wish to purchase products dedicated specifically to their needs – although they will do so if that is the only way these needs can be met. In general, they wish to purchase the same or similar kinds of products as younger consumers.

- The present over-50s generation is the first to have grown up with mass marketing and is hence somewhat cynical and hard to impress.

- Older people do not have the unifying influence of the global media and technology that creates commonality among youth. They are therefore less susceptible to the attractions of international brands and more open to national or local suppliers.

- Negative messages and social attitudes about old age prompt people to hang on to their money.

- Marketing to mature consumers benefits from an overall approach that is ethical, respects customers, recognises loyalty and provides impartial advice with good humour. Older consumers will reward trusted providers. This is the basis for relationship marketing.

The bottom line

Some experts say that there are basically two approaches to the mature market: selling 'old things' to older people or taking mainstream brands to the over-50s age group.

The former is appropriate for the specialist products and services discussed in Chapter 7. Industries currently targeting people over 50 include financial services and insurance, selected holiday providers, stair lift and specialist fixtures providers, and pharmaceuticals. For marketers, the challenge is to develop a trusted brand that does not constrain the size of the potential target market through unwelcome associations with old age. It may be possible to sell one brand of insurance to the over-50s as a group but much more difficult to market a single brand of package holidays to such a diverse sector. There may be scope for a 'retro' approach, to recapture good experiences and reactivate brand memories.

In contrast, extending the market for mainstream brands is the best approach for the inclusively designed goods and services considered in Chapter 6. Inclusivity in marketing goes with the grain of moves towards inclusivity, and against age discrimination, in other areas such as employment and health services. At worst, marketing of mainstream brands should be age-neutral. At best, it can be actively inclusive, although for this to be executed with confidence, research would need to demonstrate no likely loss of younger consumers. But inclusive marketing may not be very visible, a matter more of nuance rather than the direct approach.

Beyond the practicalities of how best to take advantage of the expanding mature market, there are more fundamental questions about the opportunities for innovation in an ageing society. We have become accustomed to living in an economy in which growth has been proceeding steadily at 2–3 per cent per annum on average over our lifetimes. But perhaps there may be some natural limit to growth as our needs are met. It may be relevant that fewer big innovations are being brought to market in recent decades, with the Internet and the mobile phone as the two contemporary examples. Otherwise, we see the refinement of established technologies, as with the motor car whose basic arrangements have remained unchanged over the hundred years of mass production that started with the Model T Ford.

Perhaps the limits to economic growth will become visible first among the buying habits of affluent older people, whose needs are satiated. The mature market is the place for solid quality and service to retain appreciated customers who value the offering, with limited scope for volume growth and innovation. The mature market is the place for those who can take on the challenges of marketing in a zero-growth society.

Further reading

Barsby, V. (1997) 'Speaking the grey language', *Admap*, September

British Code of Advertising Practice. London: ASA (see www.asa.org.uk)

Broadcasting Audience Research Board [regularly publishes television audience data with limited breakdown by age groups]

Carrigan, M. and Szmigin, I. (1999) 'Ageism in advertising – a new age for old age?' in: K. Lavery (ed). *The Definitive Guide to Mature Advertising and Marketing*. Shipton: Millennium Direct

Coleman, R. (2001) *Living Longer: the new context for design*. London: Design Council

Datamonitor. (2002) *Senior Consumers*. London: Datamonitor

Diamond, R. (2003) 'Unlocking the value of the over-50 consumer', *Admap*, May

Harris, K. (2000) 'Silver service: what drives the greying market?' *Admap*, November

Help the Aged. (2002) 'Marketing and advertising to older people'. Report of a seminar held on 19 September 2002. London: Help the Aged

Kotler, P. (2003) *Marketing Management*, 11th edition. London: Prentice-Hall

Lavery, K. (ed). (1999) *The Definitive Guide to Mature Advertising and Marketing*. Shipton: Millennium Direct

Lazer, W. (1986) 'Dimensions of the mature market', *Journal of Consumer Marketing*, vol 3, pages 23–34

Martyn, S. (1999) 'Age differences in ad responses', *Admap*, December

Millennium Research Bureau. (2003) *Mature Thinking: a social and statistical portrait of Britain's mature market*. Shipley: Millennium Direct

National Readership Survey. [regularly publishes data on readership of newspapers and magazines broken down by age]

Tylee, J. (2002) 'Why are we never seen in adverts?' *Saga Magazine*, November

Stroud, D. *50+ marketing blog*, at www.50plus.blogspot.com

Stroud, D. *Making the Web '50+ Friendly'*, at www.20plus30.com

Sylvester, S. (2002) *You're Getting Old: Europe's demographic problem is your marketing problem*. London: Young and Rubicam

Szmigin, I. and Carrigan, M. (2001) 'Learning to love the older consumer', *Journal of Consumer Behaviour*, vol 1, pages 23–34

Selected UK agencies specialising in marketing to people over 50

Diametric
www.diametric.biz

HeadlightVision
www.headlightvision.com

Millennium Direct
www.millenniumdirect.co.uk

OMD UK
16 Bishops Bridge Road, London W2 6AA

Senioragency
www.senioragency.com

20 plus 30 (use of interactive technologies in marketing to the over-50s) www.20plus30.com

10 Ten key points for business

This final chapter distils the information and ideas set out in the previous nine chapters into ten concise messages. There are also some questions, the answers to which readers might like to consider in the context of their own businesses.

1 Buy into demographic change

For business, the main implication of population ageing is that the centre of gravity of the population is shifting towards the older age groups. The mature market is the only growth market, in terms of demography. Younger market segments are static or shrinking. The number of people over 50 in the UK is projected to rise from the current 20 million to 25 million in 20 years' time. By 2020, the over-50s age group will comprise half the adult population. These are your customers, or your customers' customers.

Do you know the demographics of your product or service? And that of your competitors? If not, is it important to know?

Is the ageing population best viewed as a creeping trend, allowing a measured response in the fullness of time? Or is a more urgent response appropriate for your business sector? Can you learn from US experience, where their baby boom generation is running ahead of ours?

2 Understand income, wealth and purchasing power

People over 50 spend some £175 billion a year on goods and services. This is about 45 per cent of total consumer expenditure.

Pensioners have never been so well off (let's hope it lasts). This means that retirement is generally no big deal financially. For most, there is no great change in income or expenditure around retirement. A reduction in both by some 20 per cent on average following retirement reflects lower income offset by fewer financial obligations. New pensioners are therefore in a pretty similar position financially to late-working-age people of similar socio-economic status. (Older pensioners, who retired some time ago, are less well off, particularly single women – a point not to lose sight of.)

The financial net wealth of the over-50s age group is over £500 billion. Older people generally continue to save throughout retirement, accumulating substantial net financial wealth as well as housing wealth. A lot of this is left as bequests to family members – £35 billion a year.

Some believe that it is a myth to assume the availability of this huge wealth of the over-50s group, because they tend to hoard their assets against the uncertain prospects for longevity. Perhaps as important is the reluctance of older people to replace consumer durables merely for the sake of change, despite mostly having the income that would allow them to do so. In terms of consumption, many older people do not enjoy the living standards they could well afford. There are opportunities for marketing goods that would be seen as excellent value for money and services that provide unique lifetime experiences. The trick is to put your proposition while your customer still has an interest in spending.

There's an old joke that goes 'Why do you rob banks?' And the bank robber replies 'Because that's where the money is.' This can be translated into an ethical key point about the finances of people over 50: 'that's where the money is', even after retirement.

3 Get attuned to emerging ideas about ageing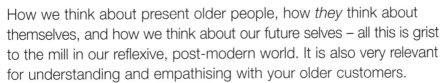

How we think about present older people, how *they* think about themselves, and how we think about our future selves – all this is grist to the mill in our reflexive, post-modern world. It is also very relevant for understanding and empathising with your older customers.

The latest shift of the cultural *zeitgeist* places emphasis on 'inclusivity' – including older people in the mainstream, whether in the realms of employment, design, retailing, advertising or marketing. In an inclusive world, capability is more significant than disability. As the centre of gravity of society shifts away from the young, and as the 'new old' become included, the prospects for the continued dominance of the youth culture are beginning to look rather uncertain. Marketing orientated exclusively towards the young may therefore be based on increasingly shaky foundations.

Inclusivity means designing, planning, managing and marketing to maximise the proportion of the population for whom the product or service is suited. Inclusivity in employment means having staff who understand their older clients, whether in designing, marketing or retailing. An inclusive approach treats older people simply as people, with no special regard paid to their age. This is an important perspective to help unlock the spending power of older customers.

So, how inclusive is your business, in respect of both those who work with you and what you sell? Are age discrimination and ageist attitudes still part of the culture? If so, can you expect to take advantage of the market opportunities of an ageing society? Is it cool to be mature in your business? If not, when will it be?

4 Understand what it's like to be old ● ● ● ● ● ●

Most older people have little in the way of discernible impairment. But disability and frailty catch up with us sooner or later, however successfully we plan to age. Our physical, sensory and mental capabilities decline, although the timing is not predetermined. We can undoubtedly delay the onset of decrepitude by adopting a healthy lifestyle throughout the course of our adult lives, and there are benefits from clean living, however late we might start. Partly through recognition of the virtues of active ageing, older people today are fitter, stronger and more capable than those in the past.

Partly because our capabilities depend on how actively we use them, differences between individuals of the same age are considerable. Older people are very variable in their capabilities, attitudes and inclinations. This limits useful generalisations about what it's like to be old. So beware of stereotypes. Yet at the same time, age is a great equaliser, with class differences in health and well-being becoming less marked as later life progresses.

Chronological age, counting the years from birth, is certainly a rough proxy for the cumulative impact of 'life' on an individual. But a better measure of our physical and mental state is how far one is away from the end of life, rather than how far from the beginning. The majority of us escape both sudden death from acute disease and the chronic degenerative conditions of later life such as Alzheimer's. For us, frailty and the need for care are mostly confined to a relatively compressed year or two in the run-up to death, regardless of the age at which we might die. Until then, most of us can expect to remain in passable health, with any luck.

Prior to the onset of frailty, we can be old but still active. So what does it mean to be old? Being old is undoubtedly a distinct life stage, in that one has experienced youth and middle age, may have been married to one person for half a lifetime, may have brought up children to adulthood, may have lost a spouse, and in the process have acquired considerable experience, not to say wisdom. Whilst some of our attitudes reflect this changing perspective, others remain largely unchanged since youth – hence the common feeling that what is odd about growing old is that you don't feel any different.

So for business, what does it mean to have older customers? First, you need to know them. Talk to them. Mix with them. Recognise their diversity. Understand their wants and needs. If you're not of their age group yourself, aim to operate across generational boundaries. Look out for differences between successive generations, for instance in attitudes to innovation or demanding good service. Avoid stereotypes and over-simplifications. Talk to those who study ageing. Commission market research.

Second, think how you could help your mature customers, and potential customers, with the things that matter most to them:

maintaining good health and physical functioning, freedom from depression, personal optimism, well-retained mental abilities, engaging in social activities, feeling supported, and living in a good, safe neighbourhood. Businesses succeed by recognising and meeting people's wants and needs. The message of this book is that many wants and needs of mature consumers remain to be met.

5 Think market segmentation ● ● ● ● ● ● ● ●

The mature market is large and diverse. To respond to its needs, segmentation into sub-markets is unavoidable. How best to do this? There are a number of approaches, each of which has its advocates and applicability. A matter of horses for courses. Here is a concise guide.

Segmentation by age group is easy and has common-sense appeal. But chronological age is not a particularly good indication of our capabilities, attitudes or interests, given the diversity of the older age groups. Perhaps the most persuasive argument is that age-based segmentation differentiates groups by reference to attitudes and habits derived from formative experiences in adolescence and early adulthood. This could be important if you're in the business of selling things with 'retro' appeal. Age-based segmentation is also relevant for financial services where the timing of the transition to retirement is linked to age (although less precisely than in the past).

Segmentation by income applies to the over-50s market as much as to any other sector. Incomes vary considerably. Affluent older people are major purchasers of new cars, of luxury goods generally, as well as of leisure and travel activities. They have time as well as money. It is common for marketing messages to be targeted ostensibly at age groups younger than the actual purchasers; for instance, the up-market car bought as new largely by people over 50 whose advertising images are all families with young children. Are such campaigns based on careful research that shows, for the specific product, that this particular marketing approach is exactly what will motivate the customer to buy? Or is there a naive ambition at work to cultivate the brand for repeat purchases, while missing the opportunity to talk to the true audience in terms that will match their concerns?

Segmentation by life stage has intuitive attractions. Although more elaborate formulations are possible, the simplest is a three-fold split:

■ entering old age, but still active and independent;

■ transitional, between healthy active life and frailty;

■ frail old age, often experienced only late in life.

Segmentation by life stage is most relevant to the marketing of goods and services that slow the transition to frailty by countering physical deterioration (nutrient supplements and exercise, for instance) and promoting independence and autonomy (home aids and adaptations, for example). Businesses already supplying specialist products and services of these kinds generally have a good understanding of their customers. But for those contemplating entering the mature market, a life stage approach, with its emphasis on health and disability, has the merit of simplicity and concreteness.

Segmentation based on lifestyle focuses on the choices that are increasingly open to people in the second half of their lives, the attitudes that drive those choices and the purchasing decisions that follow. Chosen lifestyles reflect people's objective characteristics such as health and income, together with personality characteristics such as optimism, independence, tendencies towards innovation and risk-taking, and self-sufficiency. Time is also relevant, and indeed lifestyles are shaped partly by whether consumers are time-constrained or money-constrained. Lifestyle segmentation is particularly relevant for leisure activities, holidays and travel, where the service offered can respond to the positive attributes of individuals, their elective choices as opposed their unavoidable needs.

6 Enlarge your mainstream markets ● ● ● ● ● ●

It makes obvious business sense to take full advantage of the potential of the mature market to boost sales of mainstream brands of products and services. Equally obvious is the need to manage this without alienating younger customers through generating unwelcome messages or images related to ageing. The way to handle this is through an inclusive approach to both marketing and design. Inclusive design ensures that products and services are usable by as large a proportion of the target population as is economically viable. It complements a customer-centred focus at all stages of the product cycle.

Inclusive design is good design. Generally, a consciously inclusive standpoint to design does not involve significantly higher production costs, so it might seem the obvious way to go. Nevertheless, the business case needs to be made. This will involve more than one of the product-orientated drivers of inclusive design:

■ legislation, which imposes obligatory requirements, as for instance in regulations made under the provisions of the Disability Discrimination Act 1995;

■ formal standards, particularly when incorporated into procurement requirements, as for example those forming part of the Building Regulations governing new housing;

■ customer feedback, which can be exploited in product development by customer-focused businesses;

■ competitive advantage, which can be boosted by unostentatious appeal to the full potential target market;

■ brand, which can be enhanced through a reputation for good design and corporate social responsibility.

Young and old alike, we need more 'forgiving technologies' – those that forgive us our inadequate capabilities. Word processing is a forgiving technology in that mistakes can easily be corrected, whereas the traditional typewriter is not. Forgiving technologies are inclusive technologies.

7 Make it your business to address the special needs of ageing ● ● ● ● ● ● ● ● ● ● ● ● ● ● ●

Inclusively designed products and services cannot meet all the needs of older people, particularly during and following the transition from fitness to frailty. This gap is filled by a range of assistive technologies and specialised services. These focus on particular disabilities and on needs that can be serviced by operations based in local areas.

There is enormous scope for innovation in both technology and delivery, both to help people to operate independently in their own homes and to help them to get out and about. Technical advances from other areas can be adapted and exploited, especially those involving miniaturisation and digitisation, and where economies of scale drive down unit costs. But it's not a market just for high-tech solutions. As the ads in the magazines with older readership show, there is demand at present for aids to bathing and showering, and for specialist chairs. Small and medium-sized enterprises can surely succeed if they can identify a need of an element of the older population and the means by which to meet it.

Are there technologies in your company that could be exploited in new ways to tackle disabilities? Conversely, are there technologies elsewhere that, if exploited by competitors, have the potential to disrupt your business plans?

To meet the local needs of a concentration of older people for some particular service, what might be termed a 'Third Age Business' model may have possibilities. This would involve Third Agers, who have retired from their main employment but who wish to continue to be economically active, providing a service to other Third Agers. We are talking about a business activity, not a voluntary activity but one with a clear 'pro bono' content. The 'partners' providing the service would be partially remunerated. They would receive payment but at below the market rate for the job, reflecting, on the one hand, the role of remuneration as a means to recognise effort and as an inducement to reliability, and, on the other hand, the fact that those concerned would have pension income and would want to ensure a flexible work/life balance. Partial remuneration would help ensure business competitiveness by easing cost pressures. One example of a Third Age Business might be a local car service tailored to meet the particular transport needs of older people no longer able to drive themselves and without ready access to public transport. A second example might involve the provision of 'handyman' and gardening services to those no longer able to do it themselves. A third instance might be to help in the recovery of some of the £1–2 billion a year of state benefits unclaimed by pensioners.

8 Evaluate the potential of your sector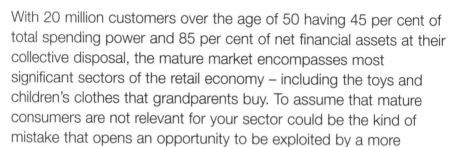

With 20 million customers over the age of 50 having 45 per cent of total spending power and 85 per cent of net financial assets at their collective disposal, the mature market encompasses most significant sectors of the retail economy – including the toys and children's clothes that grandparents buy. To assume that mature consumers are not relevant for your sector could be the kind of mistake that opens an opportunity to be exploited by a more insightful competitor.

It is not our purpose to argue that it would be virtuous or socially responsible for firms to set about meeting the needs of older people as consumers (although we think it would be). Rather, we want to make the case that there are reasonable grounds for businesses to begin to engage with the mature market, where they have not already made a start. More a matter of putting a toe in the water, as opposed to taking a plunge; moving beyond talk to put some actions in the Plan. But the necessary actions need to be addressed sector by sector, firm by firm. In Chapter 8 we discussed the prospects for a number of sectors about which we have some knowledge. But obviously we are only able to sketch out some possibilities.

Only you can identify the potential of your sector and your business, but you may need a little help. There are experts and potential partners available, ready to advise and collaborate.

9 Get to market ● ● ● ● ● ● ● ● ● ● ● ● ● ●

The design community is engaging increasingly with the concepts and practicalities of both inclusive design and the specialised assistive technologies. But the marketing community is lagging behind. Most marketing people are young, whether in the agencies or on the client side. They may have some difficulty in empathising with the inhabitants of planet maturity. There are, however, some exceptions – agencies that specialise in understanding the older consumer. You might ask, to put it bluntly, whether these people are any good. Is there a convincing case for switching from your existing agency?

In our view, the specialist marketing agencies are certainly worth talking to. The people involved have thought long and hard about the behaviours and barriers, the potential and the predicaments. They each will have their preferred approaches, in particular to market segmentation, which may be based in their own research. You will need to consider which of these various approaches makes most sense for your specific business opportunity.

But it also makes sense to see if your existing agency is getting up to speed with older consumers – some certainly are. And to enquire whether there are sources of expertise in academia and elsewhere that can be tapped. What you need are experts with knowledge both of older people and of your business sector, with whom you can have a dialogue that leads on to concrete action. Increasingly, such people can be found.

10 Drivers of change ● ● ● ● ● ● ● ● ● ● ● ●

The population is ageing. The future will be older. Families are not having enough children to reproduce themselves. Youth markets are static or shrinking. Society's centre of gravity is shifting. Older people are becoming richer and fitter. Age discrimination is on its way out.

Businesses need to address the implications of these fundamental drivers. The product range, product cycle and supply chain all need to be rethought: assessing market needs; product design to meet those needs; marketing in all its aspects; evaluating the outcome of the campaign; fine tuning, rejigging or rethinking, depending on the outcome of the first cycle. To be efficient and effective, you need people about you who understand older consumers, from designers to point-of-sales staff. An age-diverse team, including some seasoned members, makes increasing sense. Knowledgeable business partners, too. And you need to involve your older customers, one way or another. Don't second-guess their needs. They are, after all, experts in making mature choices.

About Age Concern

Older richer fitter is one of a wide range of publications produced by Age Concern England. Age Concern is the UK's largest organisation working for and with older people to enable them to make more of life. We are a federation of over 400 independent charities that share the same name, values and standards.

We believe that ageing is a normal part of life, and that later life should be fulfilling, enjoyable and productive. We enable older people by providing services and grants, researching their needs and opinions, influencing government and media, and through other innovative and dynamic projects.

Every day we provide vital services, information and support to thousands of older people of all ages and backgrounds.

Age Concern also works with many older people from disadvantaged or marginalised groups, such as those living in rural areas or black and minority ethnic elders.

Age Concern is dependent on donations, covenants and legacies.

Age Concern England
1268 London Road
London SW16 4ER
Tel: 020 8765 7200
Fax: 020 8765 7211
Website:
www.ageconcern.org.uk

Age Concern Scotland
113 Rose Street
Edinburgh EH2 3DT
Tel: 0131 220 3345
Fax: 0131 220 2779
Website:
www.ageconcernscotland.org.uk

Age Concern Cymru
4th Floor
1 Cathedral Road
Cardiff CF11 9SD
Tel: 029 2037 1566
Fax: 029 2039 9562
Website: www.accymru.org.uk

Age Concern Northern Ireland
3 Lower Crescent
Belfast BT7 1NR
Tel: 028 9024 5729
Fax: 028 9023 5497
Website:
www.ageconcernni.org.uk

Publications from Age Concern Books

Age Concern Books publishes over 65 books, training packs and learning resources. On the following pages we list some titles that may be of interest to you, or to your company. You may also be interested in customised editions of our titles, and bulk order discounts, see below and page 186.

Customised editions

Age Concern Books is pleased to offer a free 'customisation' service for anyone wishing to purchase 500 or more copies of one title. This gives you the option to have a unique front cover design featuring your organisation's logo and corporate colours, or adding your logo to the current cover design. You can also insert an additional four pages of text for a small additional fee. Existing clients include many of the biggest names in British industry, retailing and finance, the trade union movement, educational establishments, the private and voluntary sectors, and welfare associations. For full details, please contact Sue Henning, Age Concern Books, Astral House, 1268 London Road, London SW16 4ER. Tel: 020 8765 7200. Fax: 020 8765 7211. Email: hennins@ace.org.uk

Your Guide to Retirement

Ro Lyon

This bestselling book encourages everyone to view retirement as an opportunity. It is full of useful suggestions and information on:

- managing money: pensions, tax, savings, wills
- making the most of your time: learning and leisure, earning money

- your home: moving, repairing, security, raising income
- staying healthy: looking after yourself, help with health costs
- relationships: sexuality, bereavement, caring for someone.

It is an invaluable guide for people coming up to retirement, planning ahead for retirement, or newly retired, as well as for employers and welfare advisers.

£7.99

Your Rights
A guide to money benefits for older people

Sally West

Your Rights has established itself as *the* money benefits guide for older people. Updated annually, and written in clear, jargon-free language, it ensures that older people – and their advisers – can easily understand the complexities of state benefits and discover the full range of financial support available to them.

£4.99

Your Taxes and Savings
A guide for older people

Paul Lewis

The definitive annual guide to financial planning for older people, this popular book:

- is fully revised and updated
- explains the tax system in clear, concise language
- describes the range of saving and investment options available
- includes model portfolios to illustrate a range of financial scenarios.

Your Taxes and Savings explains how the tax system affects people over retirement age, including how to avoid paying more tax than necessary.

£6.99

Your Guide to Pensions
Planning ahead to boost retirement income

Sue Ward

An essential guide for people in their mid-life years who are keen to improve their pension arrangements. It explores, in detail, the main types of pension scheme – state, stakeholder, occupational and personal – and offers guidance on increasing their value. It is updated annually.

£6.99

Baby Boomers
Ageing in the 21st century

Edited by Maria Evandrou

Accessible and stimulating, *Baby Boomers* explores future policy options and makes a series of recommendations. It is essential reading for business managers, health and social care planners, policy makers and anyone concerned with retirement in the future.

£14.95   0-86242-153-5

Changing Direction
Employment options in working life

Sue Ward

Changing direction later rather than earlier in working life can be challenging – and enforced change (perhaps early retirement or redundancy) can be worrying – but it can also provide an opportunity for a new beginning in a possibly more satisfying second career. This revised and updated edition will help you to identify and find outlets for your skills, whether as an employee, a self-employed person or a volunteer. It guides you through the many steps that can be taken, including:

- deciding what you really want to do
- retraining and educational opportunities
- looking for work (employed and self-employed)
- help from the State

- sorting out your financial position
- combating age discrimination
- voluntary work.

£9.99   0-86242-331-7

Elder Abuse
Critical issues in policy and practice

Edited by Phil Slater and Mervyn Eastman

Written primarily for anyone working in the areas of health and social care – as well as for academics in relevant fields – this book provides a sound framework to explore good practice and to support the recognition, management and prevention of elder abuse.

£14.99   0-86242-248-5

To order from Age Concern Books

Call our **hotline: 0870 44 22 120** (for orders or a free books catalogue)
Opening hours 9am–7pm Monday to Friday, 10am–5pm Saturday and Sunday

Books can also be ordered from our secure on-line bookshop:
www.ageconcern.org.uk/shop

Alternatively, you can write to Age Concern Books, Units 5 and 6 Industrial Estate, Brecon, Powys LD3 8LA. Fax: 0870 8000 100. Please enclose a cheque or money order for the appropriate amount plus p&p made payable to Age Concern England. Credit card orders may be made on the order hotline.

Our **postage and packing** costs are as follows: mainland UK and Northern Ireland: £1.99 for the first book, 75p for each additional book up to a maximum of £7.50. For customers ordering from outside the mainland UK and NI: credit card payment only; please telephone for international postage rates or email sales@ageconcernbooks.co.uk

Bulk order discounts

Age Concern Books is pleased to offer a discount on orders totalling 50 or more copies of the same title. For details, please contact Age Concern Books on 0870 44 22 120.

Age Concern Information Line/Factsheets subscription ● ● ● ● ● ● ● ● ● ● ● ● ● ● ●

Age Concern produces more than 45 comprehensive factsheets designed to answer many of the questions older people (or those advising them) may have. Topics covered include money and benefits, health, community care, leisure and education, and housing. For up to five free factsheets, telephone 0800 00 99 66 (7am–7pm, seven days a week, every week of the year). Alternatively, you may prefer to write to Age Concern, FREEPOST (SWB 30375), ASHBURTON, Devon TQ13 7ZZ.

For professionals working with older people, the factsheets are available on an annual subscription service, which includes updates throughout the year. For further details and costs of the subscription, please write to Age Concern England at the above Freepost address.

We hope that this publication has been useful to you. If so, we would very much like to hear from you. Alternatively, if you feel that we could add or change anything, then please write and tell us, using the following Freepost address: Age Concern, FREEPOST CN1794, London SW16 4BR.

Index

Nicholson, Jack 42
Nike 160
Nivea creams 134
'nutraceuticals' 137–138
nutritional supplements 136–138

obesity 2, 135
Odeon cinema group 106–107
ODM UK 60
Olay: Regenerist 134
optical character recognition 113
osteoarthritis 137
osteoporosis 105

packaging 34, 129, 131
Pension Credit 11, 12, 20, 145
pensions
    gender differences 12, 13, 171
    occupational and private 10, 11,
        12, 14, 15, 18, 139
    and social exclusion 26
    state 10–11, 13–15, 16, 44, 48,
        139, 171
piano playing 38
population statistics *see*
    demographics
poverty 10–11, 12–13, 26
Powergen 147–148
Propecia 135

Queen Mary 2 108

radio 45, 110, 156, 165
Radio Times 156
rail travel 96, 103, 126
Reader's Digest 156
Regenerist 134
Rehabilitation Act 1973 (USA) 71
religious issues 42, 43, 46, 98
research projects, voluntary
    149–150; *see also* market
    research
retirement age 15–16, 44
retirement communities/homes
    122–123
Ricability (Research Institute for
    Consumer Affairs) 128, 129
robots, use of 94–95
Roche: Xenical 135
Rogaine 135

Rowntree (Joseph) Foundation *see*
    Joseph Rowntree Foundation
Royal Commission on Long Term
    Care 83–84, 88, 118
Royal Cumberland Hotel, Blackpool
    110
Royal National Institute of the Blind
    (RNIB) 113, 115, 148, 149, 153
    technical information website
        129–130
Royal National Institute for Deaf
    People 113
Rubinstein, Artur 38

Saga Group 109–110, 111, 136, 144
    advertisements 153, 160
    equity-release product 143
    radio stations 156
Saga Magazine 109–110, 155, 156
savings 19–20, 23, 55
self-care tasks 39, 89
Senior Life 155
SENIORWATCH project 70
sexual behaviour 42, 43
sheltered housing 47, 88, 90, 117,
    122–123
ShopMobility 96
shopping 60, 68–69, 89, 95, 97,
    120, 165, 166
    Internet 90, 95, 112, 148
    and mass customisation 79–80
    see also brands; consumer
        durables
shopping centres: information
    systems 97
Siemens hearing aids 87
sight loss 31, 35–36, 84
    and Geographic Positioning
        Systems 96–97
    see also glasses
Silver Surfers Day 112–113
skin care products 134–135, 151
Smart Home technology 91–93
smoking 2, 40
snooker 45
social needs 40, 95–98
software 68, 69–70, 74, 111,
    113–114
Sony 160
speech recognition software 87, 113

sport 45
stair-lifts 89, 167
standards: and design 72–73, 81, 176
statins 132–133
'structured dependency theory' 26–27
supplements, nutritional 136–138
'support ratio' 8
swimming 45

taxi concession schemes 127
technology see assistive technology products; computers; information and communication technologies; Internet
telecare 92
Telecommunications Act 1996 (USA) 71
telephones 85, 97, 98, 113, 129–130
  and cold calling 156–157
  mobile 98–99, 111, 165
telesales 156
Teletext 98
television 45, 59, 98, 102, 106, 115–116
  advertisements 151–152, 156, 157
'terminal drop' 37
Tesco: Access site 115
texting 98–99
Third Age, the 27–28, 59
  'business' initiatives 120, 177–178
toilets, adapted 89
tourism 107–110
trains 96, 103, 126
  model 105–106

'Transport Direct' 96
trans-retinoic acid 135
travel and transport 59, 62, 95–97, 107–110, 116, 120, 124–127, 151, 158
  concessionary fares 103, 126
  see also buses; cruises

University of the Third Age 27, 31

Virgin 160
vitamin supplements 136–137
voluntary activities/volunteering 27, 120, 150
voluntary sector see charities
Volvo 76

walking (as exercise) 45, 104, 124
walking aids 84, 85–86, 89
washing machines 18, 128, 129
wealth, older people's 21, 171
  housing 15, 21–22, 55
  see also income
Web Accessibility Initiative 71, 72–73
websites
  designing 71, 72–73, 114–115, 157
  on marketing 160–161
  RNIB 129–130
wheelchairs 83, 84, 95
Woman and Home 156
Woman's Weekly 156
word processing 111, 176
World Health Organization (WHO) 66, 137

Yours 155